WATER DISTRIBUTION

Barry Latham
BSc, CEng, MICE, MIWEM, MBIM

The Institution of Water and Environmental Management

The Institution of Water and Environmental Management
15 John Street, London WC1N 2EB

Preface

The origin of this handbook lies within my own early experience of water distribution management when, despite the availability and excellence of many technical and scientific publications, I found it necessary to frequently question and consult my superiors, peers and, particularly, subordinates about even the most routine situations and events with which I was confronted.

With that learning experience as a base the book, access to which would have benefited me in those days, covers some of the features of distribution management and practice not necessarily available in textbook form. It is aimed at those working within the distribution function who would wish to quickly and easily broaden their knowledge and at those not necessarily directly involved who would benefit from a short overview at a modest level of technical detail.

Finally, I wish to record my thanks for the co-operation and assistance of the Chairman and Board of Yorkshire Water Services Ltd.

Barry Latham
August 1990

Contents

1. General Introduction

The water cycle, in relation to the provision of water services, divides logically into four operational functions (Fig. 1.1):

(1) water resources and treatment;   (2) water distribution;
(3) sewerage; and   (4) sewage treatment.

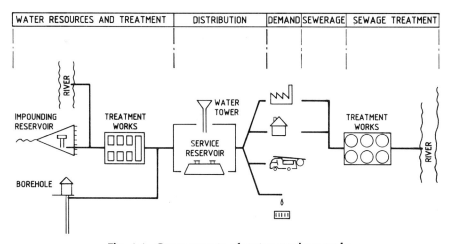

Fig. 1.1. Components of water services cycle

The distribution system embraces that part of the cycle between the reception of treated water and its delivery at the customer's tap. Management of the system is for a number of reasons a complex and sensitive process. Some of its more significant features are:

(a) The distribution system is itself dynamic; only rarely is it physically the same at the end of the day as at the beginning.
(b) The system provides a direct interface with the customer. The product appearing (or perhaps failing to appear) at the tap is a constant indicator to the customer of the quality of service received for the water supply charge in respect both of the distribution process and that which precedes it.
(c) The customer is inclined to judge the performance of the entire water service operation by the courtesy, care and efficiency of those with whom he has contact. Whilst other functions, notably the billing department, do engage in customer dialogue, it is within distribution that the most regular and widespread daily contact takes place.

The distribution system comprises a network of mains for transmitting water from storage to the customer's living or working locality together with service pipes linking mains to customer properties or premises. Such systems were evidenced as long ago as Roman times; indeed, examples of Roman water engineering and plumbing expertise are not an uncommon discovery in many towns and cities in the UK and Europe.

Parts of many existing distribution systems were constructed during that period of vigorous industrial growth in the 19th century when substantial investment in the urban infrastructure was seen as an essential ingredient to manufacturing prosperity. Our Victorian predecessors laid down the basic framework of many present-day urban distribution systems and, whilst there are mains over one hundred years old continuing to give sterling service, some of the older pipework is in need of substantial rehabilitation.

The following chapters provide an insight into some of the physical, technical, technological, scientific and managerial aspects of the distribution system and an indication of the challenges posed by organizational change in the water industry.

Bibliography

THE INSTITUTION OF WATER ENGINEERS AND SCIENTISTS, *Water Distribution Systems* (T. W. Brandon, Ed.), Water Practice Manual No. 4, IWES, London, 1984.

2. Physical Aspects

1. INTRODUCTION

This chapter describes the installations and apparatus encompassed within the distribution system.

2. SERVICE RESERVOIRS

A service reservoir is a receiving tank for treated water, situated on high ground near a centre of population; it serves three main purposes:

(1) to dampen hourly customer demand peaks;
(2) to provide contingency storage; and
(3) to compensate for variations in water quality.

Surface water sources (impounding reservoirs or river abstractions) tend to be situated where rainfall is high and where raw water is relatively unpolluted, often remote from the centre of population; groundwater sources, which may be geographically close to the population, lie deep, often several hundreds of metres below ground level. In the absence of the service reservoir, installations for providing and conveying water from source (treatment plant, transmission mains and pumps) would need to be of sufficient capacity to meet peak hourly customer demand and capable of fine adjustment as demand varies throughout the day, with capital and operating cost implications. The service reservoir facilitates a steady output from source over at least each 24-hour period and limits the 'upstream' design capacity requirement to peak day, peak week, or greater dependent upon its volume (Fig. 2.1).

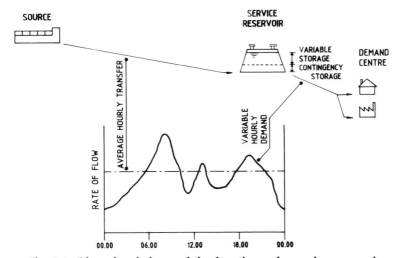

Fig. 2.1. Diurnal variation and the functions of a service reservoir

The water level in the service reservoir rises and falls throughout the day as demand varies, whilst the rate of incoming flow from source remains steady. Most service reservoirs are designed to provide a minimum quantity of contingency storage, represented by the volume remaining when the water level is at its lowest. Should a failure occur in the system upstream of the reservoir, supply to the customer can be maintained for a period pending rectification of the problem.

WATER QUALITY

The quality of water entering the service reservoir can, and does, vary according to fluctuation in raw water composition, treatment process change or adjustment to input in those cases where the reservoir is fed from two or more sources. The service reservoir by virtue of its capacity and internal design orientation provides time retention and mixing, thereby blending waters of differing quality and reducing the degree of change apparent at the customer's tap.

SIZE OF RESERVOIR

The chosen size of the reservoir depends upon a number of factors, notably the water demand placed upon it, the degree of demand variation, the risk of upstream system failure and its strategic importance (it may be linked with others or capable of supplying neighbouring zones). The reservoir may be as small as a few cubic metres in capacity or as large as 200 000 m³ or more (those containing more than 25 000 m³ in the form of above-ground storage are subject to the inspection and records requirements, for safety purposes, of the Reservoirs Act 1975), but typically a service reservoir will be designed to provide storage equivalent to 24 or 36 hours water demand from the zone it serves.

ON-SITE STORAGE

Many industrial customers provide their own on-site contingency storage; indeed, a minimum volume of local storage is a condition normally imposed upon industrial premises with a metered supply. The high-level cold water storage tank installed in most domestic properties is another form of service reservoir, providing benefits to the water undertaker through the cumulative effect of demand smoothing and to the resident as a reserve source of water should his supply be interrupted. (Domestic storage tanks represent perhaps the earliest form of service reservoir, their original purpose being to contain reserve stocks of water when primitive public supplies were available only at certain hours of the day).

DESIGN OF RESERVOIRS

Service reservoir designs are many and varied, ranging from small individual steel tanks through masonry or brick structures to those of large reinforced concrete construction. Normally the reservoir will be a covered rectangular box or series of boxes divided so that sections can be isolated for cleaning and repair, allowing the remainder to continue to function, albeit at reduced throughput or capacity. Circular tanks, often of pre-stressed concrete construction, represent economical design as individual units but occupy proportionately more land than rectangular or square tanks in a multiple configuration. A prime requirement is to ensure that the quality of water in the reservoir is protected through the prevention of ingress of contaminated water from the surrounding ground or from rainfall, by adequate security against vandalism or the entry of animal life and by an effective ventilation system to keep the water 'sweet'. A series of baffle walls are usually incorporated and input/outflow pipework arranged to produce good circulation and prevent stagnation (Fig. 2.2).

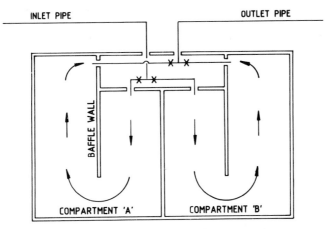

INLET PIPE   OUTLET PIPE

BAFFLE WALL

COMPARTMENT 'A'   COMPARTMENT 'B'

Fig. 2.2. Plan of typical service reservoir

3. WATER TOWERS

The water tower is a form of service reservoir, elevated above ground to artificially create height (and therefore pressure in the distribution system) usually in areas of flat topography. The water tower fulfils much the same purpose as a service reservoir, although its form of construction does impose capacity limitations and it is therefore capable of serving only relatively small zones of demand.

The tower may be accompanied by a local pump installation for filling direct from the incoming main, or in some cases from an adjacent service reservoir, the tower providing water to a high-level sub-zone to that served by the main reservoir.

Older forms of construction tended to be of massive masonry or brick with cast iron tanks, often originally unroofed, or of steel towers and tanks. Modern construction is usually in concrete (Fig. 2.3), sometimes as a slender tower with a tank of 'inverted mushroom' shape, often exhibiting interesting, if not universally appealing, architectural licence.

4. WATER MAINS

DEFINITION

A main is defined as a pipe laid for the purpose of providing a general supply of water as distinct from a supply to an individual customer.

CATEGORIES OF MAIN

There are two categories of main:

(a) the trunk main, for conveying water from source to treatment, from treatment to reservoir or from reservoir to reservoir; and

(b) the distribution main, forming part of the distribution network.

Trunk mains do not normally have branch or service pipe connections, distribution mains do.

Fig. 2.3. Examples of water towers

ARRANGEMENT OF MAINS

The distribution mains system (sometimes referred to as the reticulation system) comprises a network of pipes usually arranged in pressure zones allied to a specific service reservoir or water tower and valved such that each is divisible into smaller zones for the purposes of leakage control or district metering. Neighbouring pressure zones are often interconnected but isolated from each other by zone boundary valves which can be opened if necessary, thereby providing operational flexibility should the need arise (Fig. 2.4).

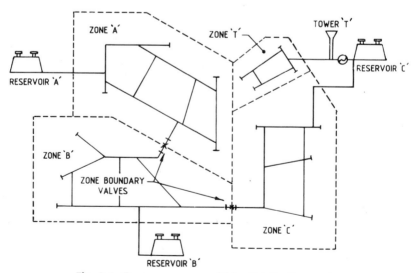

Fig. 2.4. Pressure zones within distribution system

6

SIZES OF MAIN

Mains in the network range in diameter from as small as 50 mm (2″) to 450 mm (18″) and above in some of the larger conurbations. The vast majority, however, are 75 mm (3″), 100 mm (4″) or 150 mm (6″) nominal diameter; current design practice has standardized upon 100 mm and 150 mm for most new mains, although 63 mm and 90 mm coiled plastic pipes are finding increasing favour at the extreme ends of the system, for culs-de-sac and for confined road layouts on new housing development sites.

MATERIALS USED FOR MAINS

The mains system comprises a multitude of pipe materials, cast iron, spun iron, ductile iron, asbestos cement, uPVC (unplasticised polyvinyl chloride) and MDPE (medium density polyethylene) being the most common, but there are others. The water industry has been somewhat conservative in its selection and use of pipe materials, understandably so since the provision and maintenance of mains is an expensive and long-term affair. The last ten years however have seen significant technological advances, a widening availability of choice and an increasing commercial competitiveness amongst pipe manufacturers, to the extent that designers are more willing to vary their choice, with confidence in the whole-life performance of the selected material.

MAINS RENEWAL

Typically the quantity of new main laid each year represents perhaps no more than 1–2 per cent of the length of the entire distribution system, older or less favoured materials being therefore likely to comprise the major part of the network for some time. These will continue to require maintenance, necessitating the stocking of appropriate repair fittings and a continuity of working expertise.

5. SERVICE PIPES

DEFINITIONS

A service pipe is the small diameter pipe conveying a supply of water from the main into the customer's property. The majority of service pipes are 13 mm (½″) nominal diameter, although they can be much larger, perhaps even the same diameter as the main from which they originate when supplying large industrial installations. The service is normally laid, for frost protection, at a minimum depth of 750 mm.

OWNERSHIP AND RESPONSIBILITIES

Ownership and responsibility for maintenance and repair of the service pipe are split between the water undertaker and the property owner, the demarcation between the two being designated in law as the boundary of the street within which the main is laid. In most cases this is the same as the property boundary (outer wall of the building or garden fence) at the point at which the service pipe crosses it.

The section of the service pipe for which the water undertaker has responsibility is referred to as the 'communication pipe' and the section for which the property owner is liable is the 'supply pipe'. (These definitions, contained within the Water Act 1945, are not repeated within the Water Act 1989, although the term 'supply pipe' continues to be used in the context of regulatory standards. Whilst their omission in the latest legislation may create some confusion within the industry they are for convenience retained throughout the remainder of the text). A boundary stop-tap, also owned by

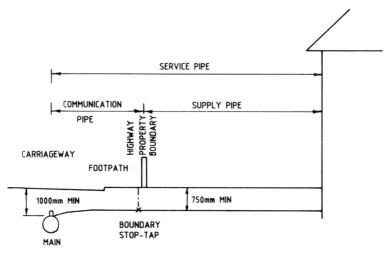

Fig. 2.5. Service pipe

the undertaker, is usually installed at the downstream end of the communication pipe, as close as possible to the boundary. The property owner usually has his own stop-tap within the building, close to where the supply pipe enters (Fig. 2.5).

Many customers are unaware of this division of responsibility, believing instead that the water undertaker's liability for maintenance and repair of the service pipe extends to a point inside the property, a similar arrangement to that applying to the electricity and gas utilities, whose responsibility, originating probably from safety considerations, extends to the internal supply meter. It is important to note that a water meter may be fitted on the service pipe (at the external boundary, within the property, or at any position in between) but its location has no relevance to the division of responsibility for or ownership of the pipe itself.

JOINT SUPPLIES

The type of service pipe arrangement shown in Fig. 2.5 is very common and is the usual form adopted in new service installations. There are however a number of more complex arrangements in existence, notably the joint supply, where the supply pipe, in joint private ownership, serves several properties (Fig. 2.6). Joint supplies are

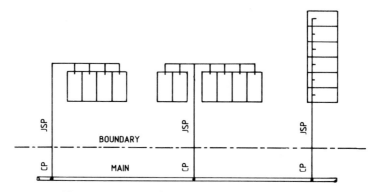

Fig. 2.6. Some typical joint supply arrangements
(C.P. – communication pipe; J.S.P. – joint supply pipe)

8

frequently found in older urban areas, a legacy in some cases of the industry's organization prior to 1974, when local authorities often had responsibility for water supply as well as housing, the whole service pipe in those circumstances being within the authority's ownership as both water undertaker and property landlord.

Joint supplies can be problematical. They tend to be old, prone to bursting and blockage, and no longer adequate to provide sufficient flow for modern-day customer water usage. They can be laid across gardens, sometimes covered by building extensions or outbuildings, or through cellars, proving almost impossible at times to locate and repair. Whilst the water undertaker has no responsibility for maintenance of the supply pipe it does have powers to persuade owners to repair leaks or even in some cases to require an owner to install, at his cost, a new separate service connection to the main.

Another situation, not necessarily involving a joint supply but very similar in terms of the problems it can present, is that where the main from which the service pipe is

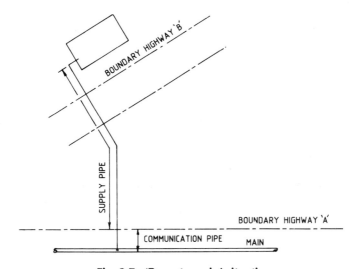

Fig. 2.7. 'Remote main' situation

taken is not in the same street as the property served (Fig. 2.7). Here the communication pipe may still be relatively short (extending only to the boundary of the street in which the main lies) but the private supply pipe can be long, laid across other streets or private land en route to the customer's property.

Complex arrangements such as these can be fraught with problems when the supply pipe is in need of attention. Statutory obligations placed upon the undertaker in respect of pressure and constancy of supply extend only to the limit of responsibility (the end of the communication pipe). Many customers are unaware that the water charge they pay covers the provision of a supply only to the boundary stop-tap, that that boundary may be more remote than the property wall, or that their inadequate supply can be the result of a defect in private pipework of which they may own only a part share. Explanation to the customer requires careful handling in such situations and can sometimes be interpreted as an attempt to evade statutory duty.

MATERIALS USED FOR SERVICE PIPES

Modern service pipes are predominantly plastic, uPVC or polyethylene, now coloured blue to conform to the National Joint Utilities Group (NJUG) colour code (gas – yellow; electricity – black; telephone – grey).

As with mains, many other service pipe materials are still in existence. Originally lead was the favoured choice for both service pipes and internal property plumbing systems but concern for health has precluded its use in recent years (practice amongst many undertakers is to replace lead communication pipes when encountered or to replace at the customer's request in situations where he agrees also to renew his supply pipe and plumbing system). Various forms of iron and copper, in the latter case sometimes coated with plastic, have been extensively used but both, particularly iron, have been liable to external or internal corrosion.

The use of plastics for service pipes has many advantages, but there are possible snags: plastic cannot be traced by electronic surface detectors unless an accompanying metal trace wire has been laid (likely to be uneconomic in most instances); care is needed therefore in positioning any new communication pipe, if feasible, at right angles to the main directly opposite to the position of the boundary stop-tap, or alternatively, to keep a record of the location of the pipe for future reference. It used to be common practice for household electrical systems to be earthed to the incoming service pipe. This has been prohibited since the 1960s by electrical regulations but of course many such arrangements still exist. Some undertakers when replacing or repairing metal services by plastic at least inform the householder that the existing earthing system may no longer be effective and that advice should be sought from the local Electricity Board; others go further in attempting to restore electrical continuity by fitting earthing straps. The situation, generally considered to be less than satisfactory, is currently the topic of national debate.

CONNECTION OF SERVICE PIPES TO MAINS

The service pipe is usually connected to the main by a ferrule positioned on the crown of the main, often inserted by an under-pressure drilling and tapping machine. A good practice when laying the pipe is to 'snake' it slightly over the length between the main and the boundary stop-tap so that thermal or ground movement is absorbed within the pipe without exerting a force on the ferrule. The boundary between the communication pipe and the supply pipe is designated by the boundary stop-tap, which may be positioned in the footpath just outside the property boundary, or just inside, in the garden, thereby saving cost. The stop-tap lies within the ownership of the undertaker, but may be operated by the customer if he so wishes. (Some older services may have no boundary stop-tap or be fitted as an alternative with a stop-tap ferrule at the main; usual practice is to install a new boundary stop-tap when these are encountered, for future convenience).

6. VALVES AND HYDRANTS

DISTRIBUTION POLICY AND PRACTICE

The movement of water within the distribution system needs from time to time to be controlled, either for re-zoning (such as accommodating changes of source inputs, or supporting demand in one locality from surplus water in another) or to isolate sections of the system for repair, maintenance, leak detection or new connections. Valves are an essential and integral part of the system: the more there are the more flexibility there is, minimizing, for instance, the numbers of customers whose supplies are interrupted when repairs and maintenance are carried out. Opinions and practices vary in respect of the number, spacing and orientation of valves. They are expensive to purchase and install and there is a delicate balance when determining policy between future requirements or risk and economic considerations (whatever the policy, significant numbers of valves in all distribution systems are installed but never operated during the whole of their lifetime).

Another variation in policy and practice relates to care and maintenance. In some cases valves are operated systematically at a set frequency to ensure that they will work if ever needed, in others little or no such routines are carried out other than perhaps on the most strategically important valves. This is another element in the prudence/economy equation.

SLUICE VALVES

The usual form of control valve is the sluice, or gate, valve containing either a wedge-shaped gate which slides via a groove cast into the valve body into a seat or, as a variant, directly on to a smooth invert, a seal being obtained by means of a surrounding rubber face. These valves are intended to be fully open or fully shut and not to be used for flow regulation (excessive wear on the valve gate can occur due to the high velocity of flow passing through the valve under partially-open conditions, thereby preventing drop-tight closure when required). It is however doubtful whether there is an inspector anywhere within the industry who has never 'cracked open' a sluice valve to satisfy a particular requirement.

On certain larger mains sluice valves may be of a smaller diameter than the main itself, tapered pipes being inserted upstream and downstream, a cost-saving practice with little adverse hydraulic effect upon the system, but in most instances the valve diameter corresponds with that of the parent main.

Most valves installed today are of the 'clockwise closing' type, but many distribution systems contain 'Waterworks Pattern', clockwise opening valves and, where there is a mixture, accurate records and the knowledge of the local inspector are of considerable value.

Valves are usually housed in a brick or concrete chamber straddling the main, often accompanied by an adjacent indicator plate with the letters **SV** and the main diameter clearly marked.

PRESSURE CONTROL VALVES

Pressures, as well as flows, within the mains system are another important consideration. The pressure at any point within the network needs to be great enough to satisfy statutory customer obligations, but significantly higher levels do no more than intensify leakage and increase wear and tear on fittings, including the customer's own water-using apparatus. Pressure reduction in such circumstances is effected by the use of a pressure-reducing valve (PRV), designed to maintain a pre-set pressure or flow in the main downstream of the valve. The modern PRV can be a highly sophisticated, electronically controlled piece of equipment capable of sensing downstream demands and upstream pressures and adjusting itself accordingly. Pressure reduction occurs most frequently in gravity-fed systems, where the destruction of energy is not uneconomic, but there are situations, for instance where a main crosses a valley and pressure at the valley bottom is higher than the minimum necessary for local requirements, when pressure reduction is not feasible owing to the need for pressure on higher ground downstream. There may be occasions even in pumped systems where pressure reduction is sensible even though energy is being dissipated having previously been generated at a cost. A typical example would be the installation of a PRV on a branch to a small community taken from a high-pressure main supplying an area some distance away.

Another, less frequently used, form of pressure control is exercised by the pressure-sustaining valve, a not dissimilar piece of equipment to the PRV (indeed a PRV can be converted to a PSV by a simple mechanical modification) but designed to protect upstream rather than downstream pressure. Typically this would be installed where water from a high-pressure zone is bled into an adjacent lower-pressure area. The valve satisfies demand to the area but progressively closes down as pressure in its own zone drops to a pre-set minimum level.

11

All pressure pipes require venting to remove accumulated air pockets or to facilitate charging. Trunk and large diameter distribution mains may be fitted with air-release valves at high points and at changes in gradient. These valves are generally unnecessary in the distribution network because of the number and frequency of service connections, through which air can be bled via the customer's taps or ball valves, and the presence of hydrants which can be opened as required when charging the system or to release any known pocket of entrained air.

FIRE HYDRANTS AND WASHOUTS

Hydrants are installed in the system either at the request (and cost) of the Fire Service or at the ends of mains for flushing or emptying. In the UK they are accommodated underground in chambers for protection against frost and other damage. Fire hydrants are clearly indicated by a yellow indicator plate affixed to a nearby wall, lamp standard or free-standing post. The plate is marked with a black letter **H**, the diameter of the main and the distance from the plate of the hydrant itself. All hydrants lie within the ownership of the water undertaker including those installed at the request of the Fire Service, which bears the cost of any associated maintenance and repair works.

7. PUMPS

ROLE OF PUMPING

Pumping is an expensive business, but has its role to play within the distribution system, for instance:

(i) For general transmission purposes (to drive water from one part of the system to another, or from one reservoir to another, or as an emergency standby for switching supplies in the event of a failure).

(ii) To fill water towers, generally from an adjacent reservoir or main (an intermittent process, normally activated by low and high water-level sensors in the tower).

(iii) For local boosting to small high-level demand points in the system. An example of this is the hydropneumatic pump, used where the relatively high cost of a reservoir or tower is not justifiable; the control mechanism is similar to that for water tower filling, pump activation being linked to pressure, rather than water-level sensing, in a small water/compressed air pressure vessel.

HIGH-RISE BUILDINGS

Requiring supply pressures often in excess of those which the undertaker is obliged to provide, high-rise buildings can at the top be at a height above that which the local system pressure will reach by gravity, requiring the installation by the owner of a booster pump at ground level to feed the building. The pump may be of the hydropneumatic type or may feed a rooftop storage tank, its operation and maintenance being within the owner's responsibility.

3. Technical Aspects

1. INTRODUCTION

Before considering work undertaken within the distribution system it is worthwhile first to examine some of the fundamental principles associated with the movement of water, an appreciation of which is vital to most operational decisions and tasks.

PRESSURE, FLOW AND PIPE FRICTION

The terms 'pressure' and 'flow' are frequently confused and often wrongly considered in isolation from each other. The movement of water in the system (rate of flow) is a result of the relationship between two key elements: pressure (the force applied to it) and frictional resistance (the inhibiting effect of the roughness of the pipe wall and fittings through which it passes). The relationship is analogous to Ohm's Law of electricity, where:

$$I \text{ (current or flow)} = \frac{E \text{ (voltage or pressure)}}{R \text{ (resistance or friction)}}$$

An increase in pressure or reduction in friction, or both, results in an increase in flow. A smaller diameter pipe exhibits a higher frictional resistance and therefore requires a higher pressure than does a larger pipe to deliver the same flow.

HYDRAULIC GRADIENT

When water flows along a pipe of uniform diameter and internal roughness the pressure falls linearly from upstream to downstream. The rate at which pressure reduces along the line of the main is referred to as the 'hydraulic gradient'. These principles are illustrated in the simple diagrammatic examples shown in Fig. 3.1.

UNITS OF MEASUREMENT

Mains pressures are normally measured in terms of metres head, either above the main or above ordnance datum, theoretically the approximate height to which a column of water would rise from a hole made in the top of the pipe. Pressure ratings of fittings are usually expressed in 'bars', one bar being equivalent to an air pressure of one atmosphere or 10.197 metres head of water.

Flow of water is usually measured in megalitres per day (Ml/d) for large mains and litres per minute (l/min) for small mains and services.

DESIGN PRINCIPLES

The frictional resistance of mains, a function of the drag exerted between the pipe

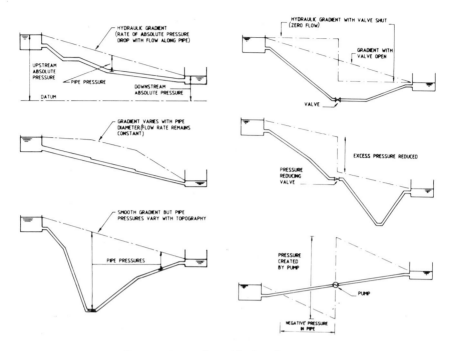

Fig. 3.1. Examples of hydraulic gradient

wall and the water travelling past it, is a much more complex matter. Hydraulic calculations used in the design of large mains are based on one of several empirical formulae available, each one of which contains a form of friction coefficient, determined from pipe roughness, age and condition. One of the most commonly used, based upon the Hazen–Williams formula, is referred to as the 'C value'. Typically a new main will have a C value of 150 plus, whereas a 50 year old main may have a C value as low as 30 through deterioration.

Generally the design process as applied to the distribution system for individual mains is rather more of a decision between, say, 100 mm or 150 mm diameters than a calculation exercise involving the use of one of the available formulae.

CUSTOMERS' PROBLEMS

Before leaving the topic of hydraulics it might be useful to reflect upon some of the situations experienced in the home by customers:

(1) Flow in the upstairs bath tap reduces when water is being drawn at the kitchen sink (because additional demand downstairs induces a higher flow in the service pipe, a greater pressure drop and less force to deliver to the upstairs tap).

(2) Plenty of water downstairs but loft storage tank remains empty most of the day (because peak demand upon the system induces a general pressure drop in the mains; the problem will occur irrespective of the condition of the service pipe).

(3) No water when neighbour five doors away waters his lawn (this is a classic joint supply pipe case, where the privately-owned supply pipe is either old and internally encrusted or undersized in relation to modern water usage, exhibiting a large pressure drop under flow conditions).

2. FLOW MEASUREMENT

REASONS FOR MEASUREMENT

There are two reasons for measuring flows: water accountability and charging. Water is a relatively modestly-priced but valuable commodity. It is inconceivable that an oil production or motor manufacturing company will not have systems capable of recording the quantities of raw materials it purchases, the number of units it produces, the volume of sales and the amount of wastage incurred in the process. The water industry is no less important and yet, with few exceptions, it is only in recent years that it has taken a truly commercial approach to the business of product accountability, unit costs and operational efficiency.

WATER CONSUMPTION

Water consumption may be categorized as:

(a) domestic usage (measured and unmeasured);
(b) industrial, commercial and agricultural usage (metered and unmetered);
(c) 'free' usage (for example, firefighting or sewer jetting); and
(d) losses (leakage, illegal use or misuse).

Categories (a), (b) and (c) are considered 'legitimate', categories (c) and (d) as 'unaccounted for', being difficult, in total, to measure accurately or calculate.

Typically consumption in a mixed urban/industrial/rural area might comprise: domestic 40 per cent; non-domestic 32 per cent; and 'unaccounted for' 28 per cent, with leakage being as much as 27 per cent of total consumption.

It is normal for source inputs to the distribution system to be measured and recorded through meters installed at the outlets from treatment works and boreholes which, together with metered imported and exported bulk supplies received from and given to adjacent systems, provide a reasonably accurate and constant measure of the total quality of water put into supply.

ACCOUNTABILITY

The purpose of water accountability is twofold: to identify and take action to minimize unaccounted for and non-legitimate usage and to ensure that future demand projections for the purpose of source and system development planning are based upon sound demand data. Ideally, wholly accurate measurement of consumption in each of the four categories of usage ((a) to (d), earlier), aggregated and reconciled with system input data, would satisfy this objective. The complexity and condition of most distribution systems, the frequency of necessary daily operational adjustments in the network, and the accessibility of the system to those who would misuse it, indicate that the full attainment of that ideal, set against its benefits, would be uneconomic.

Current practices are based in principle upon the measurement of consumption to elements of the distribution system, broken down progressively in size by districts, pressure zones, waste zones and customer premises, providing a reasonable economic optimum level of accountability. However, each elemental measuring process has been developed for its own specific purpose, for example charging or leakage detection, any attempt at reconciliation being normally accompanied by an estimated element to 'balance the books'.

METERING

Consumption within the four categories of usage is generally assessed as follows:

(i) **Domestic.** Assessed partly by direct measurement from individual metered supplies, partly by calculation on the basis of an average per capita consumption of, say, 130 litres per head per day and an average household of 2.5 persons per property.

(ii) **Industrial/Commercial.** Assessed predominately by direct metered measurement, partly by individual consumption estimate per customer.

(iii) **'Free'.** Estimated by the elimination of measured consumption, measured leakage and calculated consumption from total input plus the application of a degree of subjective assessment.

(iv) **Losses.** Leakage assessed by direct measurement, other losses by elimination and subjective assessment as above.

Meters, whether used for general flow measurement, leakage detection or charging, are available in a variety of sizes, design, capacity, sophistication, reliability and price. Care is needed in the choice of meter for the particular job, notably in respect of required flow range and maximum flow capacity. Those fitted to mains are normally accommodated within a chamber designed for ease of reading and repair or removal and in some cases may be accompanied by a bypass arrangement to maintain supply should the meter require attention. Customer meters, domestic, industrial or commercial, may be installed at the property boundary, at any point on the supply pipe or within the premises. The boundary location, necessitating a chamber, is more costly but ensures that the customer bears the charge for any leakage from his supply pipe and does avoid the difficulties in gaining access to the premises for reading or maintenance. Opinion, policy and practice regarding meter positioning vary throughout the industry (Fig. 3.2).

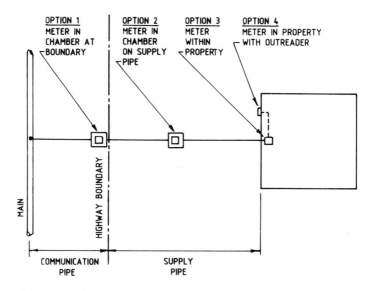

Fig. 3.2. Options for positioning meter at a customer's premises

3. GROWTH OF THE DISTRIBUTION SYSTEM

EXTENSIONS AND MODIFICATIONS

Extensions and modifications to the distribution network are constantly in progress, including:

(1) **Mains Extension** – meeting new customer demand arising from domestic and industrial building development.
(2) **Mains Reinforcement** – meeting new or increased customer demand.
(3) **Mains Diversion** – modification to existing pipework to accommodate changes, such as new road construction or building redevelopment.
(4) **Service Installation** – provision of communication pipes connecting to new customer properties.

DOMESTIC DEVELOPMENT

The provision of water to a new domestic development proceeds typically as follows:

(*a*) The local authority submits details of the developer's planning application to the water undertaker for consideration and comment. Note, however, that:
  (i) This may not occur in all cases or in every local authority area. The local authority is not obliged to consult the water undertaker as part of the planning process.
  (ii) The undertaker has a statutory duty to supply new domestic development although the developer may incur some cost and the pressure and constancy standards applicable in law to the supply relate only to properties which can be fed by gravity from a service reservoir of the undertaker's choosing.
  (iii) Comment by the undertaker may relate to a problem of site elevation, the possibility of 'off-site' mains reinforcement requirements or the presence of existing water pipes in the vicinity of the site which may need to be diverted or protected during the course of building construction. Such comment is not normally intended to influence the planning decision.
(*b*) The developer provides the undertaker with a plan of the site and preliminary details including the type, size and number of the dwellings to be built.
(*c*) Estimates are compiled of the demand from the development and the capacity of the existing distribution system to cater for the additional load. Note, however, that:
  (1) A demand estimate is normally calculated by the product of the number of properties, average household size (say, 2.5 persons) and average daily per capita consumption (120–150 litres). For particularly large developments it may be prudent to estimate peak hourly demand by the application of a factor (say, 2.5) to the estimated average daily figure.
  (2) The capacity of the existing distribution system may be estimated from field pressure and flow measurements or by simulation of the effect of the new demand using a computer model of the network.
(*d*) Off-site mains, where required, are designed and costed.
(*e*) A site mains layout is designed, materials and diameters selected, the positions of valves, fittings and hydrants designated (the latter in consultation with the Fire Service) and the requisite number and length of communication pipes to individual properties calculated. Separate cost estimates are prepared for the mains layout and the provision of communication pipes and related fittings.
(*f*) Costings are assembled, covering:
  (i) On-site and any off-site mains and associated apparatus. Note, however, that 'off-site' costs may, in England and Wales, include a proportion of the cost of any main laid up to 12 years previously within which there is spare capacity expected to be taken up by the demand imposed by the new development. (A typical case may be that in which a building development is phased over a number of years).
  Where the additional annual income generated by the new development is small in relation to mains-related costs, the developer may enter into a form of guarantee agreement with the undertaker to compensate for the financial deficit (the amount by which water charges attributable to the development are exceeded by the annual borrowing costs of a loan required to finance the mains). Such agreements may take the form of either annual payments over the following 12 years or a single commuted sum, the developer normally being given the option. A large urban development with closely-spaced dwellings is less likely to warrant a guarantee than a small estate of larger properties outside of town.
  (ii) Communication pipes, ferrules, stop-taps and meters.
  It is now common practice to meter new domestic properties since rateable values have ceased to be assigned with the introduction in April 1990 of the community charge in replacement of the local authority general rating system.

It is usual for the developer to requisition and pay for new services either individually or in batches as the building work proceeds.

(iii) Infrastructure charges, which are applicable in England and Wales and are payable usually at the same time as communication pipe charges. (See also Chapter 6, Section 3).

(iv) 'Building water' to be used during the course of construction, calculated at a rate (say £20) per property.

As an alternative, building water may be charged for by measure involving the provision of a metered connection often used later as a permanent service pipe to one of the dwellings. (The policy of general metering for all new domestic properties is likely to prompt increasing use of this method).

The developer usually pays in advance for 'unmeasured' building water. Where the measured alternative is used the pipework and meter are paid for initially, bills for water used following at monthly or quarterly intervals.

(v) 'Other' costs, for instance modifications to or protection of existing pipework affected by the new development. The developer would normally be expected to meet the cost of such preparatory works prior to commencement.

(g) A copy of the developer's plan is returned to him, marked up to show the site pipework and he is furnished with details of any guarantee agreements plus other costs and charges.

(h) Once financial arrangements have been agreed and finalized the work is planned in association with the building programme.

(i) The first task is usually to carry out any necessary off-site reinforcement work, make a mains connection onto the site from the nearest point in the distribution system, and provide a building water service connection.

(j) Progress depends upon the builder's method and rate of working. Mains are not normally laid on site until road lines and levels are set out and kerb races installed and it is rare on large developments for the whole of the mains layout to be established in a continuous operation. Communication pipes are not generally laid until they are paid for, infrastructure charges, where levied, have been met, the builder's supply pipes and plumbing systems are installed and checks for byelaw compliance have been completed.

The procedure from (a) to (j) is rarely as smooth as might be suggested. The design/cost estimation stage can be a protracted process extending over many months and requiring considerable interaction between the undertaker and the developer. The construction stage can be equally fraught, with gas, electric and telephone utilities often on site at the same time.

Undertakers are required by law to lay mains within three months of the developer's requisition and to install communication pipes within a specified period (14 or 21 days) following advance payment and byelaw approval. It is not unknown, however, to receive a builder's telephone call reporting removal vans on site, distressed new occupants and a desperate need for immediate service connections well before the allowable installation period has elapsed.

NON-DOMESTIC DEVELOPMENT

Statutory requirements regarding the provision of supplies to non-domestic development are conditional upon the preservation of the ability, current and future, to meet obligations to existing domestic and non-domestic customers.

The supply of water to new commercial and industrial development entails a similar procedure to that for domestic building but exhibits a number of differences:

(1) The non-domestic developer usually bears the cost of all on-site and off-site works. Staged or instalment forms of payment may occasionally be arranged and bonds or deposits are sometimes sought to protect the undertaker from financial losses through any default on the part of the developer.

(2) There is no equivalent 'domestic' type of guarantee agreement formally available but similar arrangements can be adopted where mutually acceptable.

(3) On-site mains and associated pipework are sometimes provided, owned and maintained by the customer, an occasional feature on small managed-unit industrial estates. The undertaker's responsibility in such circumstances terminates at the site boundary, the downstream end of the communication pipe.

(4) It is common practice for all new non-domestic premises to be metered. (On managed-unit estates, in (3) above, this may involve a 'master' meter positioned on the incoming service pipe near the site entrance and perhaps a series of private sub-meters to the individual units, the total water charge being levied upon the site manager).

(5) 'Building water' may be charged for by measure through a metered service installed to the site (often to become the permanent supply) or as a portion, say 0.1 per cent, of the construction cost.

(6) The installation to non-domestic sites can include pipework specifically for firefighting purposes and may involve dialogue between the undertaker and the site insurers with respect to the levels of pressure and flow available.

(7) All new metered customers are required to install a minimum volume of storage (normally sufficient to cover the peak 8-hour demand on the site), although such conditions may be relaxed where considered appropriate. Water-using processing companies are requested to provide estimates of average daily and peak hourly consumption at the design stage in order to identify any system reinforcement requirements and to ensure that future peaks will not 'flatten' the system and adversely affect supplies to other customers.

(8) New non-domestic customers whose supplies in any way include a 'domestic' element (such as kitchens or toilet facilities) are liable, in England and Wales, for the payment of the infrastructure charge.

Mains Reinforcement

A requirement to reinforce the system may arise for a number of reasons:

(a) To meet additional demands, as described earlier. Off-site reinforcing mains are occasionally laid in a larger diameter than that required solely to meet the requirements of the new development in order to provide some general reinforcement to the system. In such cases the marginal additional cost of the larger main is borne by the undertaker.

(b) To overcome known pressure or flow deficiencies. These may be identified from investigation following customer complaints, increases in existing demands or perhaps the necessity for over-frequent adjustments in the system to achieve supply standards.

(c) To improve circulation and reduce water quality problems. All distribution systems contain sediment or debris arising from the products of corrosion, the deposition of suspended matter or the precipitation of substances from solution. This material tends to accumulate at the extremities of the system, for instance in a 'dead-end' such as a cul-de-sac, and it is often worthwhile to connect mains in reasonably close proximity to prevent or reduce the risk of dirty water at the customer's tap.

(d) To provide a strategic link between neighbouring systems or pressure zones (for use in emergencies or to increase operational flexibility).

Mains Diversion

Highway construction or realignment, urban redevelopment or new building construction can often impinge upon existing distribution mains or networks. Arrangements are required in such cases either to protect and provide access to the affected mains or to divert them around the intended construction. The costs of such works are borne by the scheme promoter, although the financial arrangement can in some cases involve the deduction of a 'betterment' contribution in recognition that the diverted main, being new, provides a more valuable asset.

New Services

New communication pipes are laid both to serve new customer properties and to create separate services for existing individual properties in overcoming the problems of joint or shared supply pipes. These works are undertaken at the cost of the developer, customer or property owner and are usually charged for on the basis of a 'standard charge' tariff whereby the ferrule, stop-tap and up to the first few metres of pipe incur a fixed cost, an additional charge per metre being added according to overall length. Exceptionally long or difficult installations, for instance those crossing major roads, may be charged for on the basis of individual estimate.

REDUNDANT MAINS OR SERVICES

Whilst strictly misplaced in a section on 'growth', it is appropriate in the context of physical change to consider mains redundancy, when properties become permanently disused or are demolished.

Mains and services, whether 'live' or empty, represent a potential source of leakage or contamination. Sound practice is to physically disconnect any redundant main or service from the remainder of the system and, of course, to amend records accordingly.

Many networks, particularly in heavily urbanized areas, become extremely complex over the years as the number of properties and scale of demand change. Whenever work on the system is undertaken, consideration should be given to any opportunity for rationalization to reduce complexity and eliminate unnecessary pipework.

4. REPAIR AND MAINTENANCE OF THE DISTRIBUTION SYSTEM

Maintenance of the distribution system, whether of a routine pre-emptive nature or in the form of repair, is an unrelenting, costly, major aspect of operational activity. The most common forms of maintenance within each of the system's elements are described.

SERVICE RESERVOIRS AND WATER TOWERS

The retention of water in reservoirs, whether of short or long duration, incurs the precipitation of matter and the accumulation of sediment, posing with time the risk of poor quality water being put into supply and an environment conducive to the growth of micro-organisms and various forms of aquatic animal life.

Cleaning Procedures

Reservoirs require regular internal cleaning, normally to a three to five year frequency programme, the choice often geared to individual reservoir characteristics so that those known to be problematical are cleaned relatively more frequently than others.

The cleaning operation involves the emptying of one section of the reservoir (small, single-compartment tanks are accompanied by bypass pipework so that supplies, albeit without contingency storage, can be maintained during cleaning), the removal of sediment from the reservoir bottom, the cleansing of floor and walls by high-pressure jetting and the sterilization of the whole compartment prior to refilling and recommissioning. The operation is a labour-intensive task usually undertaken by a specialist team using dedicated equipment and fully conversant with the hygienic features of the exercise (Fig. 3.3).

It is common practice to position a bath of sterilizing solution adjacent to the entry point for cleaning footwear and equipment; teams are sometimes provided with overalls and boots colour coded or clearly marked to prevent their use on other less hygiene-demanding tasks. It is essential to ensure good ventilation, forced if necessary, whilst work is carried out, particularly during sterilization. Oxygen deficiency monitors and breathing apparatus may be used on initial entry to the reservoir immediately after emptying.

Inspection and Repair

The opportunity is usually taken, during the cleaning exercise, to undertake a

Fig. 3.3. Service reservoir cleaning

thorough internal and external structural inspection to identify faults such as cracks in the walls, floor and roof, blocked or defective ventilators, damaged access covers or doors. When the integrity of the roof is in doubt a leakage test can be conducted by flooding the top of the reservoir and checking for seepage from within the tank.

Minor repairs, such as the grouting of small cracks, the replacement of covers, vents or doors and the restoration of gates, fences and roadways are undertaken during the cleaning exercise, more major works being reported for later action. (Effort should certainly be made to complete all internal work whilst the reservoir is empty to avoid the inconvenience and cost of de-commissioning between cleaning operations.) Older reservoirs are prone to roof leakage, the elimination of which may require the removal of overlying earth or gravel, the sealing of individual cracks or, where the structural condition of the roof if not its impermeability is sound, the installation of a butyl rubber or similar membrane over which the surface material is replaced (Fig. 3.4).

Fig. 3.4. Installation of service reservoir roof membrane

21

Grass Cutting

Service reservoirs, because of their generally functional shape and proximity to residential areas, are frequently camouflaged by landscaping within the curtilage, including a grass covering to the wall embankments and roof. Grassed roofs are occasionally used for recreational purposes. Good housekeeping is therefore essential, not only to maintain the aesthetic appearance of the site for the benefit of local residents, but also to convey the image of care exhibited in respect of an important and potentially vulnerable asset within the public water supply system. Over-long grass in the vicinity of ventilators and openings encourages insects and other animal life and a systematic mowing programme is required during the growing season. It is usual for emphasis to be placed upon grass cutting and external work during the summer months and on internal cleaning during the remainder of the year, thereby achieving efficient deployment of the workforce involved.

Surveillance

Expansion in the use of telemetry has reduced the necessity for routine reservoir visits for water-level recording but regular attendance is still required for sampling. It is prudent for the sampler when he visits, or for the local inspector whenever he is in the vicinity, to maintain surveillance of the reservoir and its surroundings in order to check and report on external damage, pollution risk or acts of vandalism, the latter often a particular problem in certain areas, irrespective of the degree of site security provided.

DISTRIBUTION MAINS

Repair of Burst Mains

The repair of mains bursts is a regular, constant activity in most distribution systems. A typical mixed system of average age span will exhibit of the order of 30 bursts per 100 km of main in an average year; mining subsidence, high pressures, heavy pumping or a period of adverse winter weather conditions can easily double or treble this figure.

Burst mains may be identified in a variety of ways, ranging from supply failure reported by customers or telemetered alarm, routine leakage detection and reservoir level recordings, to visual evidence of ground level subsidence or flooding (Fig. 3.5). The causes of bursts or leaks can be:

    (i) corrosion of the fabric of the main;
   (ii) pressure surging (induced by pump failure or over-enthusiastic valve operation);
  (iii) ground movement through subsidence or freezing/thawing conditions;
   (iv) overloading from traffic;
    (v) joint deterioration; and
   (vi) accidental damage caused by other utility operations.

Leaks, even if relatively substantial, can remain undetected for considerable periods where, for example, pressures are high and there is no appreciable effect on customer service and where the escaping water is absorbed by receptive ground or finds its way into the sewerage system. Systematic leakage detection is described later.

Bursts in the barrel of the pipe (not at joints) take the form of small holes, or circumferential or longitudinal cracks. The method of repair is normally to fit a split collar or repair clamp around the pipe or to cut and remove the damaged section and replace with a new dowel piece joined to the existing pipe at each end, with a special coupling capable of tolerating any difference in outside diameter between the two sections (Fig. 3.6).

The actual repair work is usually a minor part of the whole operation, being accompanied by:

Fig. 3.5. Effect of burst in high-pressure main

Fig. 3.6. Typical mains repair method

(1) identification and operation of valves to isolate the affected section and perhaps re-route supplies;
(2) site preparation, including the erection of barriers, lamps and possibly temporary traffic lights;
(3) the removal of floodwater by pumping;
(4) penetration of the road surface, excavation and exposure of the pipe; and
(5) system recharging, backfilling, road reinstatement and site clearance.

Structural failure at pipe joints is uncommon (evidence suggests that joints represent the strongest parts of a pipeline) and joint leaks are generally the result of decomposition or deformation of flexible sealing inserts, usually of lead, rubber or plastic, used in making the joint. Repair work may comprise the remaking of the joint, the installation of an overlying repair collar as a replacement joint, or the removal of a section of pipe containing the defective joint and the insertion of a new dowel piece. The recording of mains failures, including location, type, ground condition, depth, diameter, material and state of the pipe, is a sound practice for compiling general information about the system, for pinpointing specific problems, or for providing evidence in deciding whether the main has reached the end of its useful life and should be replaced.

Bursts and leakage resulting from mining subsidence are inevitable, despite precautionary measures such as material selection and the provision of flexible joints. Close and continuous liaison with the mining industry is essential since the costs of subsidence-related burst repairs are recoverable, though often entailing protracted and difficult negotiations.

Maintenance of Mains

'Maintenance' in the context of underground pipework has tended to be reactive, in response to failure such as a burst or a known hydraulic or water quality-related problem. Pre-emptive maintenance has been relatively unusual principally because knowledge of the condition of buried pipes has been less than comprehensive. Some undertakers began during the 1980s to invest in general rehabilitation of older parts of the system on the assumption that old mains not necessarily exhibiting symptoms of distress, would, within a relatively short time, become problematical.

In order to reduce the 'firefighting' element so prominent in practice most of the industry has introduced, in association with privatization, 'Asset Management Planning' in respect of underground mains and service pipes, a system of condition assessment and priority ranking based upon sample analysis of the system within a framework of zones. Its objective is to establish maintenance/rehabilitation pro-grammes to beyond the year 2005 for the purpose of achieving standards of service.

Apart from bursts and leakage repairs the scope of work associated with mains maintenance and rehabilitation is illustrated by Table 3.1, set out in increasing order of complexity, effectiveness and cost.

TABLE 3.1. **Some Works Associated with Mains Maintenance**

Relative effectiveness	Technique	Problem	Typical cost (£/metre)
Short-term	Flushing Swabbing Air scouring	Water quality	0.3 0.6 1.0
Long-term	Renovation	Water quality/ hydraulic deficiency	15–25
	Renewal	As above and/or structural weakness	35–100

Cleaning of Mains

Mains flushing is the simplest technique used where pipework orientation has led to an accumulation of sediment at a particular locality. Cul-de-sac and other 'dead-end' mains are common examples, the process of sediment removal being simply to open the end hydrant, thereby increasing the velocity of flow and allowing water to run to waste until it clears. The exercise may be undertaken on a routine basis for a known chronic problem or for a specific purpose – for example, following a customer complaint.

Swabbing is undertaken in those cases where the simple process of sediment removal by increasing flow velocity is insufficient to achieve the desired result, typically where the deposited material is attached to the pipe wall. The method involves the insertion

24

into the main, usually via a hydrant, of a plastic foam swab of slightly larger diameter than the internal pipe bore. A downstream hydrant and an upstream valve are opened, the swab being driven by water pressure along the affected length. Whilst the process can be effective it does require an interruption in supply, the swab can occasionally become stuck due to a constriction in the pipe, requiring excavation for its recovery, or the swab can be ripped apart if the pipe walls are heavily encrusted.

Air-scouring, suitable for mains up to 200 mm diameter, is a more vigorous process than flushing or swabbing, using a mixture of compressed air injected through an upstream hydrant and water bled through a partially-opened upstream valve. The method can be very effective on heavily encrusted mains or for overcoming problems of animal infestation, the air/water mix being able to penetrate and dislodge material unreachable by a passing foam swab. The success of the operation relies upon the skill and experience of the operator in achieving the most effective air/water balance, often by trying a range of flows indicated by turns of the upstream valve and visually examining the colour of the water discharged at the downstream hydrant. Air-scouring is so energetic that significant quantities of encrustation from the pipe wall may be removed during the exercise which, whilst hydraulically beneficial, can expose bare metal, accelerate corrosion and possibly lead to 'bleeding' of oxidized iron and the appearance of rust at the customer's tap.

The processes of flushing and swabbing are temporary, short-term, perhaps repetitious, solutions to water quality-related problems not necessarily associated with the structural condition of the main itself. Air-scouring is less likely to be repetitious, often used as a means of prolonging financial investment but considered short-term in comparison with the more major works of mains renovation or renewal. Considerable quantities of water may be wasted during the course of all three operations.

Renovation of Mains

Renovation is undertaken where the hydraulic performance of the main is substandard and/or its internal condition adversely affects the quality of water and where the fabric of the pipe wall is considered on examination to be sound enough to withstand the process itself and provide adequate extended life. Examination may take the form of the removal of one or more sample pieces from the main, shot blasting off-site to expose the core metal, and inspection for signs of tuberculation or other structural weakness. The process of renovation comprises two stages:

(a) internal scraping for removal of encrustation and the achievement of a smooth wall finish; and
(b) the application of a new wall lining, usually of cement mortar or epoxy resin, providing corrosion inhibition and a hydraulically smooth finish (Fig. 3.7).

Fig. 3.7. Main before and after scraping and lining

Renewal of Mains

Any structural weakness within the fabric of a defective main requires its renewal, traditionally by provision of a new main in parallel, the transfer of service pipes and the abandonment of the old main. There are however a number of cheaper, more technologically sophisticated, renewal methods currently available, based on the principle of direct replacement, thereby reducing road excavation and reinstatement costs. Two popular techniques are:

(i) **Pipe Bursting.** This is a technique whereby a bullet-shaped burster, attached to a uPVC sleeve, is winched by cable through the old main. Once the sleeve is in place an MDPE inner pipe is pulled through to form the new main. Excavation holes are required only at each end of the main and at intermediate service connection points. The new main laid by this process can be the same diameter as that replaced, or even slightly larger if required.

(ii) **Pipe Swageing.** This is a method similar in principle to the renovation technique of scraping and lining, but rather more of a strengthening and renewal than relining process, in which the main is first scraped and a new MDPE sleeve, normally preheated, is squeezed into a smaller diameter, winched into the old main and allowed to expand and reform. The new main is a composite of the plastic sleeve supplemented by the residual strength and characteristics of the older pipe.

These newer techniques are most successfully deployed on long straight lengths of main with relatively few service connections, their economic advantage diminishing with increasing numbers of bends and obstruction hazards and the necessity for frequent service connection excavations.

Pumping Plant and Valves

Pumping plant and automatically-controlled valves such as PRVs are (or should be) regularly maintained on a planned basis to prolong efficient life and minimize the risk of breakdown. Standby or duplicate units may be installed to accommodate both routine and breakdown maintenance works without recourse to the interruption of supply.

Practices vary in respect of manually-operated flow control valves, of which there may be thousands in a typical distribution system. Routine maintenance of all valves is unlikely to be cost beneficial. A good inspector will appreciate the comparative importance of the valves in his district and develop a routine for systematically operating those he considers the most valuable to ensure that each will effectively open or close should the necessity arise (sluice valves left open for protracted periods may prove difficult to close if, for instance, debris has accumulated in the gate seating; those left shut can seize with time, requiring great force to move and the risk, as a result, of spindle deformation or fracture). Broken valves are seldom repairable *in situ*, necessitating replacement involving a mains shut-down and consequential inconvenience to many customers. Another frequent but less serious problem is leakage from the gland in the bonnet of the valve through which the spindle passes; this can be overcome on site and without a supply interruption by renewal under pressure of the gland packing material.

Fire Hydrants

Fire hydrants are routinely tested by the Fire Service. Defects associated with the hydrant itself, or its chamber, cover and frame or the identification post and plate, are reported to the water undertaker for the purpose of carrying out the repair, the cost of which is subsequently recharged to the Fire Service.

Service Pipes

Repair of Leakage

Service pipe maintenance extends predominantly to that section of the service for which the undertaker is responsible, the communication pipe, including the ferrule connection to the main and the boundary stop-tap. Such maintenance is generally unplanned in nature and is more likely to be prompted by leakage detection, customer complaint of low flow, or a localized water quality-related problem.

Communication pipe leak repairs represent a significant proportion of daily workload, particularly in older areas of the system and during adverse winter weather. Repairs can often be undertaken, without the necessity to shut down the main and interrupt supplies to neighbouring properties, by using a freezing kit to stem the flow for a period sufficient to complete the work. Interest in respect of leakage extends also to the privately-owned supply pipe, statutory powers enabling the undertaker to demand that repairs are promptly carried out either by private plumber or by the undertaker, the costs of which are rechargeable to the owner. Supply pipes can be isolated (provided of course that there is a working boundary stop-tap) or frozen and repaired without the necessity for a main shut-off, although other properties may be affected in the case of a joint supply. It is important to remember that the property occupier has the right to operate the boundary stop-tap for his own purposes.

Flow Standards

It is usual to adopt an 'adequacy of flow' standard for service pipes, typically of the order of 12 l/min at the first internal draw-off tap in the property (almost always the kitchen sink cold tap) and 22 l/min at the boundary stop-tap (greater in the case of joint supply pipes serving two or more properties). The difference between the two standards takes account of the pressure loss in the pipe between the boundary and the property under flow conditions.

Undertakers in England and Wales are obliged to declare these and other standards, to publicize them to customers in the form of a Code of Practice, and to monitor and regularly report performance to the Director General of Water Services.

'Poor Supply' Procedure

On receipt of a 'poor supply' complaint an inspector will check the flow at the first internal tap, using a simple flow measurement can (Fig. 3.8) or hand-held meter with hose connector (he may also check mains pressure and/or flow at the nearest available hydrant, although an individual complaint is unlikely to be indicative of a more widespread system problem). Where the tap flow is considered substandard the next

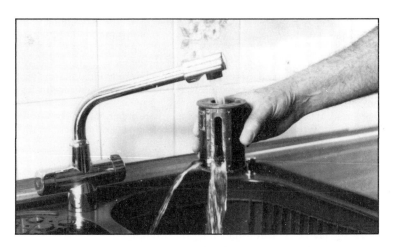

Fig. 3.8. Measuring flow at tap

step is to excavate at the boundary, expose and cut the service pipe as close as possible to the stop-tap (this may require a mains shut-off) and measure the flow. Exposure of the communication pipe affords the opportunity to determine its material, diameter and condition, information pertinent to the subsequent decision whether to clean or replace if the boundary flow is inadequate. Prior to taking further action it is good practice at this stage to expose and clear the ferrule connection to the main. Blocked ferrules are a common cause of poor supply and, unless an extensive main shut-off or a difficult road excavation is involved, ferrule clearance may provide a simple solution to the problem.

Clearance or Replacement of Communication Pipes

Where the communication pipe is considered capable of continued life and suitability it may be cleaned to improve flow. The process is essentially one of forcing water by portable pump from the boundary back into the main, the reversal of flow loosening and removing any debris or encrustation, sometimes supplemented by the injection of compressed air, similar in action to the air-scouring method of cleaning mains. A previously popular practice, now little used for hygienic reasons, was to insert a lump of bread into the pipe as a swab, it being dispersed and 'lost' on entry into the main. On completion the boundary flow is remeasured and, if adequate, the pipe is reconnected and the internal first tap flow checked. Should this remain below standard the customer is advised to attend to the supply pipe, although supply pipe cleaning, with the owner's consent, is sometimes attempted in the interest of good public relations.

Communication pipe replacement policies vary between water undertakers, some electing to renew all pipes of lead, galvanized iron or other now unused material, particularly where the main is on the same side of the road as the property and the pipe is short. Failure of the cleaning process, evidence of corrosion or insufficient depth of cover may also prompt renewal, even for 'long-side' connections.

Water quality problems, particularly discolouration or suspended matter, are predominantly caused by poor mains condition or the orientation of the main in relation to the property affected. It is usual following such complaints to flush the main and request that the customer opens the first property tap until the water runs clear. Occasionally this proves to be unsuccessful, necessitating recourse to cleaning of the service, relocation of the ferrule connection to the main, or even replacement of the communication pipe to achieve the desired improvement.

Joint Supplies

The joint supply, a single communication pipe connected to a number of supply pipes serving multiple properties, can prove extremely troublesome in all aspects of service repair and maintenance. Lack of awareness and appreciation of the divisions of responsibility for the system, ignorance of the pipework layout, neglect of private pipework and disparity of standards of supply enjoyed by individual sharing customers, are typical difficulties encountered by the water undertaker when faced with service pipe problems.

Leakages in joint supply pipes can be particularly problematical. The cost of repair works, instigated by the issue of a legal notice to the several owners of the shared pipework, is recharged proportionately either to all of the owners concerned or to those connected downstream of the leak (practices vary). Recovery of costs can be a difficult and protracted process, especially from those whose supplies appear normal irrespective of the leak.

Rectification of a defect in a communication pipe connected to joint supply pipes may well achieve an adequate standard of supply at the boundary, in compliance with the undertaker's statutory obligations, but fail to improve the supply to at least some of the customers involved. This situation leaves two options:

(1) to request that the customers connected agree to share the cost of supply pipe renewal;

or
(2) to suggest to dissatisfied customers that they individually fund the provision of a new exclusive service pipe linking the main to their particular property.

Both solutions are difficult to achieve (other than perhaps in the case of local authority-owned property): although statutory powers enable the undertaker to insist upon separate services in those circumstances, such powers are rarely fully exercised. Whether the customer is faced with a financial contribution or he elects to put up with his substandard supply, his opinion of the undertaker is often poor, arising from a fundamental but erroneous belief that the general water charge covers the provision of his supply at the tap rather than at the boundary.

METERS

Whether used for water accountability, leakage control or charging purposes, meters are required to be accurate in measurement. Working parts wear with age and mechanisms become blocked with debris and sediment, nearly always resulting in 'slow' registration (recording a lower volume than that actually passed), a particularly undesirable situation in relation to revenue meters.

Repair and Replacement of Meters

Smaller diameter meters (25 mm (1″) and under) are renewed when they become defective, the old unit often being disposed of as scrap, where it is a less costly practice than repair. Larger meters are normally replaced with new or reconditioned units, the originals being repaired off-site and returned to stores for subsequent use. Very large meters are sometimes repaired *in situ* and those of greatest importance may be changed on a planned basis to ensure consistent accuracy and maximum revenue income.

Accuracy and Testing of Meters

The law demands that revenue meters (those serving customers who pay by measure) operate within an accuracy tolerance of 5 per cent. It is not an infrequent event for a customer faced with a large bill for water services to challenge the meter accuracy, in response to which the meter may be removed for testing (in his presence if desired). The cost of the test if normally recharged to the customer if the accuracy is proven to be within the legal limits. (It is ironic perhaps that failing meters, whilst incurring no test charge, are usually under-registering and the replacement meter at the customer premises, being accurate, will produce an increase in future bills).

LEAKAGE CONTROL

Sources of Leakage

All distribution systems leak; typically some 25–35 per cent of water put into supply is wasted. Service reservoirs, mains, communication pipes, supply pipes, customer plumbing systems and fittings are all potential sources of leakage.

Waste Detection Policy

The amount of time and effort put into the process of waste detection and system repair requires careful assessment and varies according to circumstances, the objective being to optimize the economic benefits of leakage control and the cost of its implementation (in all systems there is a 'threshold' level of leakage, the benefits of any further reduction being outweighed by the cost of its achievement).

Benefits of Leakage Control

The benefits of effective leakage control are:

(a) **Cost Savings.** Water lost through leakage has had to be procured, treated and possibly pumped on its way to the customer. The unit cost of this production/transmission process, expressed as a price per cubic metre, is known as the marginal cost of the particular supply and is used in the process of evaluating the leakage control policy.

(b) **Damage Reduction.** Undetected leakage may cause flooding or underground erosion, the latter a particular problem where roads and footpaths may be undermined.

(c) **Demand Limitation.** Legitimate demand for water is constantly increasing. Wastage represents an artificial addition to demand which, if unchecked, may lead to an economically undesirable early investment in sources, treatment plants, distribution systems and pumping plant.

(d) **Customer Service.** 'Borderline' standards of pressure and flow, experienced for instance at properties situated on high ground or at the extremities of the system, are sensitive to changes in demand upstream, where uncontrolled leakage can lead to unnecessary problems for the customer.

(e) **Integrity of the System.** Holes in the system represent a constant potential source of contamination. Whilst theoretically a pressurized system is unlikely to facilitate ingress, pressure may reduce during system adjustment or from an hydraulic effect such as surging.

Costs of Leakage Control

The costs associated with leakage control comprise the investment required to establish the process (surveys, meters, valves, records etc) and the recurring annual commitment to surveillance, monitoring, recording and repairs.

Methods of Leakage Control

There are two forms of leakage control:

(i) **'passive'**, whereby no action is taken until leaks become apparent through, say, signs of surface water, low pressure problems or customer complaints; and

(ii) **'active'**, in which leakage is routinely and systematically pursued.

Common practice within the industry is the deployment of active leak detection methods, supplemented by *ad hoc* action where leaks are identified through normal system surveillance.

Active leakage control requires that the system be divided into isolated or separable zones, valved and metered so that an accurate measure of zone consumption can be made. There are essentially two forms of measurement:

(1) **District Metering.** This is a 'relative measurement' practice in which a district zone is established, isolated from the remainder of the system and initially searched for leakage and repaired. This establishes 'base' consumption which is thereafter routinely monitored weekly or monthly by means of a district meter installed in the main feeding the zone. Subsequent searches are undertaken when consumption data indicate a short-term increase or longer-term drift in consumption relative to the original base measurement.

(2) **Nightline Metering.** This is an 'absolute measurement' method, usually involving the formation of relatively small zones, say of 1000–2000 properties. The practice is not dissimilar to that of district metering except that consumption is measured only at night, when demand is at its lowest, and it is not a continuous process. Following zone establishment the base net minimum night flow is calculated as the sum of known metered trade consumption and a domestic element, assessed from the number of properties multiplied by a selected acceptable night consumption per property expressed in litres per hour. The chosen rate per property, later used during monitoring as a target, depends particularly on the marginal cost of water to the zone and may range from, say 10 l/h per property for 'cheaper' water to 6 l/h for the more expensive.

Actual night consumption (nightline) is monitored at monthly intervals or greater, the average domestic consumption per property being recalculated and compared with the target on each occasion. Leakage tests are prompted when the target is exceeded.

Zone sizes and the actual practices deployed within these two principal methods may vary and in some circumstances a combination of both is considered appropriate. Neighbouring nightline metering zones, specifically those which are 'tight' (that is, the condition of mains and services is such that leakage is minimal and stable) may be amalgamated to form larger zones or converted to district zones requiring lower cost of monitoring whilst preserving confidence in their integrity.

Identification of Leakage

Whichever method is adopted the secondary process of identifying the sources of leakage, usually carried out at night, is broadly similar, based upon progressive sub-division of the district or waste zone and remeasurement by mobile or *in situ* meters capable of measuring low flows. This exercise (step-testing) requires that the zone be equipped with valves, meters or metering points arranged in such a way that the test always follows a pre-set pattern and can be described in the form of a zone instruction sheet requiring minimal familiarization for any new team undertaking the operation. The pinpointing of specific leaks requires experience and skill upon the part of the inspectors involved. 'Sounding' (the use of a sounding bar or stick) remains as popular and effective as it was when first introduced a hundred years or more ago; the expert inspector can, by positioning the stick on a fitting attached to the pipe under test, establish both the existence of a leak and its approximate location by interpreting the noise of running water audible through the earpiece (Fig. 3.9). There are a number of electronic devices available for acoustic testing, for example the 'leak noise correlator' (Fig. 3.10), their use becoming greater as they develop but still requiring skilful operation and interpretation of results.

Repair of Leakage

Any leakage control policy is as good only as the quality and speed of the follow-up repair activity. Similarly the importance of accuracy in the process of detection cannot be overstated; unfruitful excavation for the purpose of repair (known as a 'dry hole') is time consuming and expensive and can negate much of the good work which has gone before.

5. MAINLAYING

PLANNING AND DESIGN

Distribution mains are generally laid in road, carriageway, footpath or verge and may en route take the form of self-supporting pipe bridges or be accommodated within existing bridges spanning roads, railways or rivers. Site conditions can be problematical in terms both of the negotiation or avoidance of obstructions and existing underground apparatus and of the disruption to traffic flow and general inconvenience due to the construction process.

Work planning in respect of these site difficulties is, or should be, an integral part of the design process, the culmination of which is ideally a complete scheme dossier including details not only of the route, diameter, length, material, qualities and cost estimate for the new main and its associated apparatus but also the construction methodology, location of existing underground installations (involving consultation with other utilities), traffic flow and diversion arrangements and programme of work. The requirements of the Public Utilities Streetworks Act 1950 (PUSWA) demand that notice of intention is provided to the local highway authority at least 28 days in advance of the commencement of work.

EQUIPMENT AND MANNING

The majority (about 80 per cent) of the time, effort and cost involved in mainlaying comprises the excavation, backfilling and reinstatement of the trench, the actual laying and jointing of pipes being a relatively straightforward and speedy operation. Site equipment typically comprises an excavator/loader, a crew vehicle equipped with the

Fig. 3.10. Leak noise correlator

Fig. 3.9. Sounding for leakage by listening stick

necessary tools for the job, a towed or on-board compressor and messing facility and a lorry for transportation of pipes and fittings, surplus spoil and, where appropriate, imported fill material. An essential piece of equipment worthy of special note is the electronic cable locator, used to pinpoint live cables prior to digging (Electricity Board records are not necessarily any more precise than those of the other utilities). Modern locators are reliable and accurate but capable only of detecting current-carrying cables; potted-end 'spurs' and lighting cables (during daylight hours) cannot be located by this means (Fig. 3.11). The size of the crew is dependent upon the nature and complexity of the job but teams of two men are often all that is necessary.

Fig. 3.11. Use of cable locator

EXCAVATION

Before excavation commences it is usual to assemble pipes and fittings on site, sufficient to maintain progress but not so much that they represent a hazard to the public or provide too tempting an opportunity for theft and vandalism. The increasing use of plastic pipes in coils or light straight lengths, with greater ease of handling and transportation, minimizes the need for on-site storage of large quantities.

The traditional method of excavation in a carriageway involves first the breaking of the hard wearing course by compressor-driven pneumatic drill and then trenching by mechanical digger. The trench must be deep enough to provide 1 m cover above the crown of the pipe when it is laid, wide enough to facilitate pipelaying and good compaction of fill material but as narrow as possible to minimize cost. The trench may be widened at the position of each pipe joint to provide adequate working space. The trench bottom is prepared by rough levelling and the removal of any protruding rocks or debris followed by the installation of a layer of sand or other fine granular material to form a smooth bed on which the pipe is to be laid.

The actual pipelaying mode of operation varies with the pipe material and chosen method of jointing. Ductile iron pipes, in standard 5.5 m lengths, are manually handleable at 100 mm diameter but larger diameters require mechanical lifting, usually by the excavator/loader, excavation being halted whilst the machine is engaged in the task. Sleeved spigot and socket joints are used for straight pipelaying lengths, the excavator backacter arm being used to push each pipe into place. uPVC pipes of the same standard length are similarly jointed but due to their relatively light weight do not require mechanical lifting. MDPE pipes are jointed electrothermically by butt fusion or electrofusion using specialist equipment. These may be in coiled formation (up to 150 mm diameter) or in straight lengths to a maximum of 12 m, requiring in either case relatively fewer joints. The jointing process can be carried out on the surface adjacent to the trench, the pipe being 'snaked' into place as excavation progresses (a more continuous operation, the excavator not being required for pipe lifting or jointing – Fig. 3.12). It is usual when laying plastic mains to install a plastic-coated metal mesh strip in the trench to facilitate future location of the main.

Fig. 3.12. MDPE pipe jointing

Valve and hydrant installations and end or intermediate connections to other mains usually involve the provision of flanged or other bolted joints, associated fittings and pipework often being assembled above ground, or even off-site and lifted mechanically into position. Pipes need from time to time to be cut to length on site, a simple hacksaw operation when using plastics, but a major job in the case of ductile iron, requiring the use of a motorized rotating pipe cutter. Sluice valves and bends may be surrounded in concrete to prevent movement from thrust and the possibility of joint springing.

BACKFILLING AND REINSTATEMENT

It is usual to discuss and agree with the highway authority, prior to commencement, the nature and quality of backfilling and trench reinstatement. Backfilling is done in layers around and above the pipe, original excavated material being used if it is considered suitable, otherwise by using imported fill. Each layer is thoroughly compacted by vibratory roller or rammer and the road surface temporarily restored in the form usually of a hot-rolled bitumen-based wearing course, left slightly proud of the surrounding road surface to accommodate any settlement. After a period of several months the highway authority removes the temporary wearing course and sub-base (the depth removed being dependent upon the quality of material and workmanship) and installs a new permanent surface, the cost of which is recharged to the undertaker.

The business of temporary and permanent reinstatement is costly and relations between the utilities and highway authorities can have their problems. Standards and arrangements agreed with one highway authority or individual area inspector may not be achievable in another; water utility and highway authority boundaries are often not coincident, resulting possibly in the adoption by a water undertaker of differing reinstatement practices in different districts. To be fair the situation can be equally as fraught for the highway authority in relation to the several utilities with which it deals. The problem has been recognized nationally, the subject of a committee study culminating in the publication of the Horne Report[1], which recommends many changes intended to rationalize procedures, the main theme of which suggests a shift of responsibility for permanent reinstatement from the highway authority to the excavating utility. The report has been received with general approval on all sides and is likely to prompt new or modified parliamentary legislation.

NEW TECHNIQUES

High reinstatement costs have focused attention upon 'no dig' or 'minimum dig' techniques of mainlaying, typical examples of which are:

(a) **Directional Moling** – a system suitable for smaller diameter mains – in which a guided boring head attached to a cable is hydraulically driven at a shallow angle down through the road surface to pipe depth, levelled out, travelled the requisite distance and directed upwards to penetrate the road. The end of the plastic main, preferably in coiled form, is attached to the cable and winched in the reverse direction into place. Reinstatement is required only at those points where the mole enters and leaves the road and at service connections.

(b) **The Mainlaying Train** – an extension of the use of one of the numerous trenching machines currently available – capable of speedily cutting a clean narrow slot in the road and

Fig. 3.13. Mainlaying by narrow trenching train

removing spoil. Careful selection and deployment of ancillary plant and equipment in a 'train' formation following the excavator can produce a continuous integrated laying process achieving rates of up to 300 metres per day in highway, including excavation, pipelaying, backfill and reinstatement. Some highway authorities are prepared to accept the completed work as permanently reinstated, resulting in a significant cost saving to the undertaker (Fig. 3.13).

Mains Testing

On completion of laying, the new main, whilst isolated, is filled with water and hydraulically tested by pumping to a pressure 50 per cent above estimated maximum working pressure. Measurements are taken of any pressure drop over a period of several hours, together with the volume of water pumped into the section of main to restore test pressure. Excessive amounts in either case can indicate leakage which, in the absence of any visible evidence, may necessitate a test repeat on each of two halves or further sub-divisions of the main. A peculiar feature of MDPE pipe is its tendency to creep under pressure, making it difficult to achieve test pressure stability, particular care in the testing process and a greater tolerance of apparent loss being required.

Sterilization

After hydraulic testing the main is emptied, flushed or swabbed, refilled with chlorinated water and allowed to stand for a number of hours. It is then again drained and charged for supply purposes whilst still isolated. Water samples are taken for bacteriological analysis, on successful completion of which the line valves and stop-taps are opened and the main put into service.

A good standard of hygiene is essential throughout the course of the work. A visual inspection of pipework and fittings for cleanliness prior to installation, the plugging of open pipe ends during periods between jointing, the removal of any groundwater from the trench bottom and general site tidiness are simple and cheap habits which may prevent a subsequent bacteriological test failure and the costly repeat process of flushing, swabbing, sterilization and test.

6. SERVICE LAYING

'Service laying' is the term generally used to describe the process of installing new or replacement communication pipes.

Methods of Excavation

Properties on new estates usually necessitate the provision of mains and services prior to completion of the road surface, involving laying in 'unmade ground'. Excavation in such circumstances is relatively inexpensive and quick, communication pipes being normally laid either manually or mechanically by 'cut and cover' method to a depth somewhat shallower than the final minimum 750 mm cover requirement, allowing for eventual road formation.

Communication pipes to properties fronting an existing highway may be laid by one of a number of available moling techniques requiring only a driving pit above the main, used initially for the purpose of installing the ferrule, and a reception pit at the boundary, used lastly for the location of the boundary stop-tap and chamber. Successful moling requires that the route is relatively free of underground obstructions, necessitating the appraisal of other utility records prior to commencement.

Where the developer intends to complete road construction after mainlaying and in advance of the installation of services, prior arrangements may be made to provide plastic ducts across the road through which single or multiple pipes can be fed, avoiding the need for excavation. Resultant cost savings may be passed on to the developer in the form of a discount on the price of the new communication pipes.

Ferrules are usually inserted 'under pressure' to avoid the necessity to empty the main, interrupt supplies to existing customers and incur the risk of contamination. Stop-taps are installed in a chamber constructed of precast concrete units or a vertical plastic tube, the latter easily cut to length to position the chamber cover accurately flush with the road or ground surface. Combined stop-tap and meter boxes are becoming popular with the prospect of charging policy changes.

Blue MDPE is now the most common material for both communication pipes and supply pipes, sawn to length and jointed electrothermally or by simple mechanical unions.

Communication pipes are not usually laid and connected until the developer has installed the property supply pipe, has had it checked for depth and has paid in advance for the new connection (and, where applicable, the appropriate infrastructure charges). This practice provides obvious safeguards but the increasing practice of developers to use coiled MDPE provides the potential for mutual economy through either the undertaker or the builder laying the whole of the service from the property to the main, the undertaker making the ferrule connection. Any arrangement allowing the builder to lay the whole service would of course require some terms of agreement to ensure compliance throughout with the byelaws.

7. DISTRIBUTION SYSTEM RECORDS

LEGAL REQUIREMENTS

It is a legal requirement that records are kept of all mains and that they are updated following new mainlaying or modification. The maintenance of service pipe records is not mandatory but is practised in some areas and can prove extremely useful although in general the costs involved in provision, storage and updating are likely to exceed any benefits.

The Water Act 1989 stipulates that mains record are updated 'as soon as reasonably practicable' after completion of work, whereas previous legislation in England and Wales stipulated a maximum period of six months. The 1989 Act requires also that mains records be made available 'at all reasonable times' for inspection by the public free of charge.

The accuracy of mains records varies throughout the industry and it is fair to say that the standard of most is considered unsatisfactory to the degree that the 1989 Act also obliges undertakers to improve records of existing works by the year 2000.

FUNCTIONS OF MAINS RECORDS

Mains records serve a number of purposes:

(i) a basis for system planning and design;
(ii) for use in day-to-day operational work and emergency situations; and
(iii) an information source in dealing with planning, PUSWA-related or other external enquiries.

METHODS AND PRACTICES

The format of 'manual' mains record systems based upon Ordnance Survey Maps comprises generally a master set of negatives, large scale for the more complex urban systems (1:1250 or greater) and small scale (1:2500 down to 1:10 000) for mains in rural areas. 1:10 000 (or 6″ to 1 mile equivalent) was the smallest scale allowable by law. The Water Act 1989 does not stipulate a minimum scale requirement (in acknowledgement perhaps of the industry's move toward the adoption of digital mapping) but this omission is unlikely to prompt any significant departure from former 'manual' practices. The master record is kept at a strategic location with drawing office facilities, duplicate prints in negative or paper form being stored at other operational locations (such as depots) where frequent access is required. Site survey data in respect of new, altered or abandoned mains are fed into the records office and transposed on to the master negative, conforming generally with the standard of detailing referred to as STC 25^2, a continuous task for the staff involved. Amended sheets are reprinted and distributed to other locations either instantaneously or in batch form, say every 3 months, depending upon the extent or importance of the amendment. Some undertakers keep duplicate microfilm copies of the master records both for routine use via screen magnification and for security purposes in the event of fire or accidental damage affecting the original sheets. The value of accurate and up-to-date records cannot be over-emphasized, errors and omissions often resulting in inefficiency, costly mistakes or damage to underground apparatus.

Inspectors usually keep their own 'field book' detailed records of the part of the system under their control which, together with local knowledge acquired sometimes over many years, represents a mine of useful information often not available from formal records. A wise practice when an inspector leaves his job is to at least recover his field book if not to subject him to intense questioning in an effort to elicit some if not all of his personal knowledge.

DIGITAL MAPPING

Manual mains record systems are now being superseded by digital mapping, a computerized system of recording exhibiting many advantages:

(1) **Capacity.** Digitized records comprise a series of computer files in 'layered' format, capable of storing large amounts of additional information such as burst history, customer complaints, pressure or leakage zone data and able quickly to reproduce only the specific details sought through a particular enquiry.
(2) **Ease of Updating.** Records are amended by the use of keyboard or 'mouse' compared with the laborious task of draughting and tracing.
(3) **Speed of Reproduction.** Duplicate recording systems are instantaneously updated via computer links, saving time and effort in printing and transporting paper copies. Access to records in the field via a vehicle-mounted terminal is a likely further development.
(4) **Compatibility.** Digitized records provide the potential for linking with other computer-based systems such as network models, leakage control or even the record systems of other utilities, the latter having the potential to simplify and expedite PUSWA-related enquiry requirements.
(5) **Security.** Disk data storage is less susceptible to damage or loss and can be duplicated with minimal effort.

8. REFERENCES

1. HER MAJESTY'S STATIONERY OFFICE, *Roads and the Utilities (Review of the Public Utilities Street Works Act 1950)*, Report to the Secretary of State for Transport by a committee chaired by Professor M. R. Horne, HMSO, London, 1985.
2. DEPARTMENT OF THE ENVIRONMENT/NATIONAL WATER COUNCIL, *Sewer and Water Mains Records*, Standing Technical Committee on Sewers and Water Mains, Report No. 25, 1980.

Additional Bibliography
3. DE ROSA, P. J., HOFFMAN, J. M. AND OLLIFF, J., *Pipe Materials Selection Manual*, Water Authorities Association/Water Research Centre, London, 1988.
4. DEPARTMENT OF THE ENVIRONMENT/NATIONAL WATER COUNCIL, *Leakage Control Policy and Practice*, Standing Technical Committee on Water Regulations, Report No. 26, HMSO, London, 1980.

4. Technological Aspects

1. INTRODUCTION

This chapter examines some current and future applications of new technology within the distribution function.

2. NETWORK MODELLING

A House of Lords Technical Committee recommendation that capital investment in the water supply infrastructure should be evaluated and justified by computer-based analysis has led, together with the increasing availability of high quality software, to a great deal of activity throughout the industry in the field of network analysis and modelling.

The hydraulic characteristics and behaviour of a single main are relatively simple to calculate manually, using one of the several empirical flow formulae available. The distribution network, however, is much more complex; the effects of an additional or abandoned main can be far-reaching in respect of pressures and flows. Manual analysis of networks is an iterative, laborious, time-consuming task reliant very much upon the skill, experience, judgement and often guesswork of the engineer, carrying the risk of inaccuracy and the possibility of financial or operational error.

Computer-based modelling has been available for several decades, early forms being of the analogue type, limited in scope and housed in large space-consuming cabinets containing a maze of valves and electrical wiring. These have been superseded by digital methods, of infinitely greater capacity, sophistication and speed of action, based upon a number of bought-in packages such as WATNET[1] and GINAS[2], both of which have now reached their fourth or fifth generation of development and improvement.

The uses of a network model include:

(1) **Problem Analysis**. Hydraulic or water quality-related problem analysis; evaluation of alternative solutions through simulation.
(2) **Reinforcement/Rehabilitation Analysis**. Determination of the effects of system extension or modification; minimization of investment requirements.
(3) **Demand Growth**. Assessment of the effect of new demands and determination of reinforcement requirements.
(4) **System Failure**. Simulation of the effect of a burst, pump failure etc; determination of action required, such as re-zoning, standpipe or bowser location to maintain temporary supplies.
(5) **Energy Conservation**. Assessment of pressure or pump optimization possibilities or options.

Network model development requires firstly a thorough physical analysis of the system, using mains records and field surveys, the process of which usually identifies anomalies in the records requiring correction. This is followed by calibration, a combination of estimation and field data gathering in order to analyse the behavioural characteristics of mains in the network, including friction coefficients, pressures and flows (many a closed valve, and hence the solution of a chronic problem, has been discovered in this part of the exercise). Once the model has been constructed in basic

39

format it must be validated to ensure that not only is the physical network faithfully reproduced but that its behaviour is accurately reflected in model simulation. Validation can be a slow, difficult exercise but vital to the value of and future confidence in the model.

Reference was made earlier to the dynamic, ever-changing, nature of the distribution system, in terms of its physical features and the water demands placed upon it. A network model, accurate and useful at the time of completion and validation, will lose its integrity rapidly unless adequate maintenance is undertaken. As with mains records, models are as useful as their accuracy permits, necessitating constant and disciplined updating of data as system characteristics change. Despite the closest attention, however, errors and inaccuracies do creep in with time and it becomes necessary periodically, perhaps every three to four years with complex urban models, to undertake a complete re-validation.

Network models represent a significant investment, costing typically £1.50–£2.00 per property covered, a total outlay of say £750 000 for a network serving a city of a million population. Maintenance costs represent only a marginal addition to those already incurred for the updating of mains records but re-validation, perhaps as frequently as every three years, can be as costly on each occasion as 50 per cent or more of the original investment, depending upon the extent and quality of routine maintenance. The benefits gained from the use of models are not always apparent (who can say whether a particular new main would have involved more expense without computer analysis, or whether time and effort in dealing with a failure would have been saved without model simulation?) but it is generally believed within the industry that the adoption of modelling technology and its potential integration with other high technology processes will ultimately benefit the customer in respect of value for money and the achievement of standards of service.

3. DATA AND TELEMETRY

REQUIREMENTS

A fundamental prerequisite of distribution operations is information. The speed and accuracy of data gathered from the system are directly proportional to the efficiency of day-to-day operational adjustments and, when stored for subsequent analysis, sound data provide an essential decision base for system growth, rehabilitation and other major modifications. Such data can be divided into three categories:

(a) status – information about what is happening;
(b) failure – problem notification; and
(c) security – site surveillance.

TRANSMISSION OF DATA

Technological advancement is reducing the dependence upon manual information gathering methods, with their high costs and 'human error' aspects, manifesting itself in the form of telemetry, a generic term used to describe the process of measurement and data transmission from site to a remote manned or computer-intelligent location for the purpose of prompting action or the storage of information for future analysis.

Most modern telemetry systems relay data from site outstations via leased, exclusive or shared, telephone lines (the PST network), via radio links or, at the high technology extreme, via satellite. Data are often collected at intermediate gathering stations before onward transmission to the final destination. A common variant, either supplementary to or embodied within a more comprehensive system, is the 'dialalarm' facility by which an alarm signal, activated by a predetermined status limit at site, is communicated by an automatic telephone call to the manned location; alternatively, by use of a unique site telephone number, status data can be abstracted by similar means. A system of coding is used for this process, messages received being manually translated into a meaningful format.

USE OF DATA WITHIN DISTRIBUTION

Some examples of data source and usage within distribution are:

(i) **Service Reservoirs**
Water level status (current situation plus archive potential for trend analysis).
High and low level alarms (remedial action).
Televisual surveillance (security).

(ii) **Pumping Plant**
Pump status (current situation; sets running and on standby).
Suction and delivery pressures (operational monitoring).
Flows (operational monitoring; abnormal demand indication).
Failure alarm (remedial action).

(iii) **Automatic Valves**
Valve status (operational monitoring).
Upstream and downstream pressures (operational monitoring).
Failure alarm (remedial action).

(iv) **Flow Meters**
Instantaneous reading (operational monitoring).
Integrated flows (archive for analysis).
High flow alarm (remedial action).

(v) **Depot/Stores**
Televisual surveillance (out-of-hours security).
Intruder alarm (action).

Telemetered status data may be displayed visually in the form of a 'mimic diagram' or from a menu of multiple diagrammatic simulations via a VDU (Figs. 4.1 and 4.2).

Fig. 4.1. Telemetered information

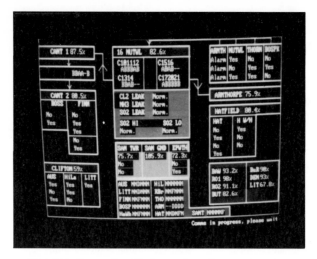

Fig. 4.2. Example of information shown on VDU

As technology develops, specifically in relation to the increasing capability and usage of site data loggers for the abstraction and storage of flow and pressure information, there is great potential for growth in the volume, quality and flexibility of telemetered data. 'Real-time' system simulation and control, linking telemetry, network models, automation, leakage control and digital mapping, is considered, within the next decade or two, to be a distinct possibility.

4. CONTROL AND AUTOMATION

APPLICATION WITHIN THE DISTRIBUTION SYSTEM

The extent to which automation and remote control are applied within the distribution system is normally somewhat less than that associated with treatment processes and perhaps some of the more major elements of bulk water transmission. Current applications in distribution tend to comprise individual pump or valve installations (particularly PRVs) and occasional more comprehensive usage in specific zones, often linked to a research and development project.

The degree to which control and automation might be applied in general throughout distribution is the subject of varying opinion and much debate. It is certain, however, that future application policy will be dictated by economic considerations, represented by the optimization of the three key parameters of technological capability, manpower and cost. Each parameter is influenced by the others and affected by circumstantial change in a dynamic relationship (Fig. 4.3).

The adoption of control and automation in distribution, with its several interdependent facets, represents a major financial investment. Each element of the system (reservoir, valve, pump etc) requires a careful cost/benefit assessment to determine both its inclusion or exclusion and, where included, its optimal arrangement.

Automatic and remote control represent the quickest and cheapest means of implementing action arising from change signified by the abstraction and analysis of data. In simple terms the action taken consists of the stopping, starting or adjustment of flows and the adjustment of pressures and is effected by the operation of valves or pumps in the system.

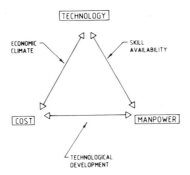

Fig. 4.3. Key parameters of control and automation

Automatic and Remote Control

Automatic control may be of the 'closed-loop' type, in which a valve or pump is operated by a local on-site arrangement of sensor, intelligent outstation and actuator, the resulting action normally being communicated for information purposes to a manned centre via a telemetered signal. Remote control takes the form of manual or computer-driven operation of switches etc from a distance following the receipt and interpretation of telemetered data and normally extends to no more than the stopping and starting of pumps or the operation of strategic valves.

Examples of Automation

Typical examples of automation are:

(1) a pump standby arrangement whereby a reserve pump is activated should a duty pump fail;
(2) a PRV capable of measuring upstream pressures and adjusting itself to regulate delivery pressure or flow at a constant level; and
(3) a water tower booster pump activated or stopped in response to a signal from a water-level sensor in the storage tank.

Manpower Requirements

In determining the scope and extent of control and automation it may be convenient to work to the simple concept of 'minimum manpower', a situation in which employees comprise only those who undertake tasks beyond present technological capability plus those who repair and maintain the technological systems installed. This represents a simplistic approach consistent with the trend of falling technology costs and rising pay; care needs to be exercised to avoid over-sophistication and complexity, resulting in task-related manpower savings but an overall net increase in costs arising from the necessity to employ perhaps fewer but more highly skilled and expensive personnel to service the installed technology.

5. REFERENCES

1. CREASEY, J. D., STIMSON, K. R. *et al*, *A guide to water network analysis and the WRC computer program WATNET, Parts I, II and III*, Technical Report TR 177, Water Research Centre, 1982.
2. LEICESTER POLYTECHNIC, *Graphical interactive network analysis simulation (GINAS) – a modelling technique and software development*, 5th edition, Leicester Polytechnic, 1989.

5. Scientific Aspects

1. EFFECT OF DISTRIBUTION SYSTEM ON WATER QUALITY

By virtue, since 1985, of the European Community Drinking Water Directive and, subsequently, the Water Supply (Water Quality) Regulations 1989, the customer is entitled to receive water for domestic purposes which is 'wholesome' – that is, complies with certain bacteriological, chemical and aesthetic standards.

The Regulations, which cover sampling frequencies, sample analysis and a requirement to keep a public register of results, lay down standards in respect of a number of parameters related to water after treatment, water in service reservoirs and water in the distribution system. It is also deemed to be a criminal offence to supply water 'unfit for human consumption'.

The issue of water quality, and public awareness of it, have during the 1980s assumed great significance. Much attention has however been paid over the years to the treatment of water at source and it is fair to say that most waters put into supply in the UK exhibit a good standard of quality in most respects; indeed, many treatment works are being uprated or refurbished to produce water complying with or even exceeding current requirements.

Regulatory standards relate also to the quality of water at the customer's first draw-off tap (after transmission through his own part of the service pipe) which, in some instances, falls somewhat short of the mark. The distribution system (service reservoirs, water towers, mains and communication pipes), together with 'private' pipework (supply pipes and internal plumbing), cannot and do not enhance the quality of water put into supply following treatment; all too often the quality is adversely affected in the process of delivering to the customer.

2. BACTERIOLOGICAL QUALITY

The water industry, with its physical and organizational features, has its origins in the days when waterborne disease was rife. Bacteriological quality was then, and is now, the prime cause for concern and attention in the exercise of procurement, treatment, storage and delivery of supplies. Bacteriologically the standard of water supplied in this country is as good as (and in many cases better than) that achieved elsewhere in the world, due in part to the nature of our infrastructure, the prevailing climatic conditions and, perhaps most significantly, the degree of vigilance and the attention to hygiene by operational staff. The distribution system is, however, vulnerable to bacteriological contamination in several ways.

SERVICE RESERVOIRS AND WATER TOWERS

Sources of Contamination

Defective access covers and leaking roofs, walls or floors are sources of potential contamination arising from the ingress of rain, surface water or groundwater. Previous mention has been made of uncovered service reservoirs (of which some are still in

44

use), which tend to provide an ideal haven for birdlife, particularly seagulls, which have developed the habit of feeding at tips or sewage works, often many miles inland, pausing for rest and relief at what represents an attractive water space en route to the next tip or back to the sea. Uncovered service reservoirs in industrial areas, because of a lowering of pH value by 'acid rain', can result in plumbosolvency (the tendency of water to absorb lead from pipework and plumbing systems).

Uncontrolled grass or plant growth brings with it animal life in the form of rodents and insects. Structural defects can in the former case lead to urinary or faecal contamination and, in the latter, entry of the insects themselves, particularly in those circumstances where air vents are broken or unprotected.

Preventive Methods

The integrity of the structure, a regular cleaning and inspection programme and a high standard of site housekeeping are essential requirements without which the risk of bacteriological contamination may be unacceptably high. In those cases where the structure must remain substandard for a period pending, for instance, some major capital investment (the uncovered reservoir is a typical example) a 'secondary sterilization' arrangement is often installed at the outlet from the reservoir.

Failure

The bacteriological failure of a service reservoir or water tower water sample requires remedial action, its extent dependent upon the seriousness of the analysis result. A 'minor' failure may prompt a re-sample, examination of which, if 'clear', is generally indicative of an initial sampling fault. A repeat failure could necessitate the addition to the reservoir of a pre-calculated dose of sterilizing solution and a retest or, at the most serious extreme, isolation and emptying of the tank for cleaning and sterilization.

MAINS AND SERVICE PIPES

Sources of Risk

The reticulation system is considered, when under pressure, to be almost free of risk from bacteriological contamination. As previously indicated, all pipework systems leak to a degree and there is a school of thought which suggests that contamination can occur from the surrounding ground through the entry of bacteria against the positive pressure. The theory is somewhat speculative and difficult to substantiate by factual evidence but it must be said that apertures do represent a risk, for instance when pressures fluctuate, and are not conducive to good hygienic practice.

The major risk in relation to pipework occurs when a new pipe, either main or service, is laid and exposed prior to connection to the existing system or when pipework is depressurized and emptied for the purpose of carrying out a repair.

Sterilization

New or refurbished mains are cleaned, sterilized and bacteriologically tested before commissioning. New services are usually connected to the main 'under pressure', pipes and fittings ideally having been cleaned and washed with a sterilizing solution beforehand. Most undertakers have procedures for sterilization in relation to repair works but their enforcement can be difficult, many such operations being carried out unsupervised or under trying conditions, where the speed of restoration of supply can perhaps have overriding priority. A useful 'backstop' arrangement when these circumstances prevail is to advise customers to boil water prior to consumption, pending water sampling and analysis.

Backsiphonage

Work undertaken by property owners, or plumbers acting on their behalf, in connection with the installation of, or modification or repairs to, private pipework and fittings, is not considered to pose a particular threat to the quality of water used in the property concerned. The industry is, however, through conditions imposed in the byelaws (see Chapter 6), obliged to ensure that the public mains system does not become contaminated by backsiphonage, a phenomenon in which water from the property can be drawn back into the main under certain hydraulic conditions.

Storage Tanks

Whilst property plumbing installations are considered generally safe, customers are advised not to drink water drawn from any tap other than those connected to the pressurized part of the system (normally the kitchen and bathroom cold taps). Others, for instance hot water or bath taps, are usually fed from the property storage tank which, being normally uncovered, is a potential source of contamination.

EMPLOYEES

Whilst considering the topic of bacteriological contamination it is important to refer to the role of employees whose jobs bring them into contact with potable water and the apparatus used for its conveyance.

Hygiene and Medical Screening

It is prudent to ensure not only that working methods are hygienically designed but that employees themselves are medically screened, particularly on recruitment, to establish that they are not carrying, or likely to be carriers of, any contagious disease such as typhoid (carriers may not necessarily exhibit symptoms of this type of condition, or even contract it themselves at any stage). Another sensible practice is to encourage employees who become ill to inform their doctor of the nature of their work and to arrange, in the case of any form of enteric infection, a series of tests, allowing a return to work only after the achievement of satisfactory results.

Requirements for Contractors

Manpower resources are not confined to those directly employed. Contractors engaged on potable water schemes are normally required as part of the conditions of contract to submit evidence of medical screening for each of their own employees.

3. CHEMICAL QUALITY

The substances with which water can become contaminated as it passes through the distribution system are numerous, the commonest being iron, manganese and lead.

IRON

Iron picked up in the system may originate from ferric hydroxide deposition or be a product of corrosion from old unlined iron mains or those in which the internal lining has been damaged.

There is an EC maximum acceptable concentration for iron of 0.2 mg/l but it is considered as rather more of a nuisance to the customer than a hazard to health. Its presence, in quantities as low as 0.1 mg/l, can impart an unpleasant, bitter, taste to water and it can precipitate out of solution in the form of minute particles when exposed to the air. The domestic spin drier is a particularly effective means of filtration for iron particles, fabrics being dried acting as a filtration medium, producing predictable and unwelcome results.

MANGANESE

Iron and manganese represent in terms of water quality the 'twin evils' of the distribution system, manganese being a more latent source of trouble and a considerably greater problem to the customer.

Manganese is not absorbed directly from pipework but minute quantities in solution leaving the treatment works, even at levels well within the prescribed EC maximum acceptable limit of 0.05 mg/l, can precipitate out in the presence of chlorine or at high pH levels to form a black crystalline deposit of manganese dioxide within the mains system. Significant quantities may accumulate over a period of years, eventually to emerge, often for no apparent reason, at the customer's tap in the form in extreme cases of a totally black liquid.

LEAD

Lead is a cumulatively toxic substance, the effects of the ingestion of which are well-publicized. The EC maximum concentration of lead at the customer's tap is 0.05 mg/l.

Whilst lead pipework is no longer installed, either by the industry or by plumbers and builders, there remain, and will remain for some years, significant quantities of lead in the form of mains joints, service pipes and fittings and lead-based solders used in the jointing of copper pipework (the use of the latter is now in contravention of the byelaws).

In some parts of the country water at source may be naturally plumbosolvent, for instance soft, peaty, acidic waters and certain hard waters derived from underground aquifers. These may require correction by the addition of lime and/or phosphoric acid prior to contact with the reticulation system. Generally, however, the risk of lead absorption from the mains network is low, although unacceptably high concentrations are occasionally encountered in older properties, particularly in the first morning draw-off from the tap, when water has been static in the plumbing system overnight.

The major risk occurs when lead pipework has been disturbed or repaired and the protective coating of lead oxide formed naturally with time is removed, leaving bare metal exposed to the water surface. Most undertakers adopt a policy of replacement, rather than cleaning or repair, in respect of lead communication pipes but it is possible that cheaper maintenance options may prevail amongst property owners or plumbers acting on their behalf.

GENERAL MEASURES AGAINST METALLIC CONTAMINATION

The presence of iron, manganese and lead is frequently associated with old pipework and fittings. As previously mentioned many distribution systems, particularly those serving urban and industrialized areas, are in need of extensive rehabilitation partly because of hydraulic deficiency and partly due to water quality-related problems of the type described. Solutions requiring major capital investment are not achievable quickly and short-term measures, such as mains flushing, swabbing or air-scouring, may have to be taken in the interim to improve substandard supplies.

4. AESTHETIC QUALITY

The customer expects and is entitled to clear, wholesome water at the tap. A supply of poor appearance may well be perfectly safe to consume but to the customer is seen as unpalatable and often regarded as a danger to health. Colour, turbidity, taste, odour and animal infestation are all undesirable and can all emanate from the distribution system.

Colour

Colour problems usually occur through the presence of peat-derived humic substances in the water at source and can be overcome by effective treatment methods. Absorption of colloidal substances (usually iron or manganese-based compounds) from service reservoirs or mains can impart colour to an otherwise clear water but this is not normally regarded as a prime problem, often being accompanied by some more obvious particulate matter.

Turbidity

Turbidity is a measure of the clarity of water, which can deteriorate through the pick-up of sediment in service reservoirs and mains (particularly 'dead-end' arrangements) or through the take-up of particles of iron or manganese as previously described.

A common customer complaint is 'milky' water, a form of turbidity due not to the presence of extraneous matter but to the appearance of entrained air, a characteristic perhaps of the hydraulics of the local main or service pipe or a temporary occurrence following system recharge on the completion of pipework maintenance. A glass of 'milky' water will usually clear completely from the bottom upwards if left to stand for a few minutes.

Taste and Odour

Tastes and odours are sometimes obvious in origin, for instance where chlorine residuals are higher than normal, but frequently their source is difficult to trace. Multiple complaints may originate from sedimentary deposition in the mains or local service reservoir or from inadequate reservoir circulation, but individual customer problems are more likely to arise from a dirty service pipe or internal plumbing system or even the use of cooking utensils of a particular material. Isolated tastes and odours may occur due to the absorption through the walls of plastic pipework of volatile petroleum-based substances present above or in the surrounding ground.

Animal Infestation

Infestation of the distribution system by minute forms of aquatic life is an infrequent but, to the customer, extremely unpleasant occurrence. Most systems suffer the problem to a greater or lesser degree at some time and the eradication process can be a difficult, costly, exercise taking perhaps weeks or even months to complete.

Types of Infestation

The most common forms of infestation include asellus (water louse), nais worms, chironomid larvae (bloodworms) and daphnia (water fleas). The point of entry is usually via an open water surface such as an uncovered service reservoir or one exposed to the ingress of organisms in terrestrial form. Entry to the mains system is generally at the egg stage of development, these subsequently hatching into larval form or, in the case of asellus, as the final stage of growth.

Eradication of Animal Infestation

Identification of an infestation outbreak, usually through the receipt of customer complaints, is normally followed by a 'bag sample' survey of the mains system. This involves a pattern of hydrant flushing at pre-selected points, samples being obtained by attaching a fine mesh bag at the standpipe outlet to filter out any foreign bodies. Information on the numbers and types of animals found is logged and the geographical extent of the problem determined.

Removal may involve a systematic programme of mains flushing, swabbing or air-scouring, accompanied where necessary by chemical dosing with chlorine or natural or synthetic pyrethrins as a means of stunning or killing. Certain species of chironomid are capable of reproduction within the mains, demanding vigorous and thorough action to effect a long-lasting solution.

5. WATER QUALITY REGULATION AND MONITORING

Water samples are taken for routine bacteriological, chemical and physical analysis from service reservoirs, water towers and sampling points in the distribution system, both fixed and random (including customers' taps), in accordance with regular programmes. The Water Supply (Water Quality) Regulations 1989 stipulate national conformity regarding sampling locations, frequencies (variable locally with recent failure history) and the various parameters for routine sample analysis.

Indicative of the level of importance attached to water quality is the extent to which the undertaker's performance in supplying water may be scrutinized, by (among others):

(1) **The general public** (a register of drinking water quality data must be prepared, updated and made available on request).
(2) **The Department of the Environment** (via its Inspectorate of Drinking Water Quality).
(3) **The local authority** (which is required by law to 'keep itself informed' about *inter alia* the wholesomeness of water supplied in its area and to notify the undertaker of any unwholesomeness with which it becomes aware. The undertaker is similarly obliged to inform the local authority – and district health authority – of any threat to water supplies in the context of a potential risk to health).
(4) **The European Community** (whose quality standards are embraced by the Water Supply (Water Quality) Regulations 1989 but to whom any member of the public or action group may choose to direct an enquiry, response to which would be directed at the UK government but would nevertheless impact, albeit indirectly, upon the undertaker concerned).
(5) **In England and Wales, the Director General of Water Services** (who is entitled to demand information on any aspect of the undertaker's activities).

Whilst water undertaker and local authority responsibilities are governed by statute it has always been good practice to maintain close liaison and dialogue with the appropriate Environmental Health Officer. Most undertakers communicate known problems, particularly those of an unusual or widespread nature, or those allegedly causing illness, to the EHO as soon as they become apparent.

6. Managerial Aspects

1. LEGAL REQUIREMENTS

Statutory obligations and provisions are too complex and voluminous to examine comprehensively here but it is useful to consider some key elements of particular influence in the management of the distribution function.

The Water Act 1989

This came into force on 1st September 1989 and applies specifically to the industry in England and Wales in the context of water privatization but does embody certain amendments to Scottish legislation, specifically in relation to water quality. It contains a number of important distribution-related features.

Supply for Domestic Purposes

Section 40 requires the provision by the undertaker of a mains supply for domestic purposes within three months of request, subject to certain conditions imposed upon the requisitioner.

Section 41 requires the requisitioner to make an annual financial contribution, where appropriate, over a twelve year period, equivalent to the difference between the water charges accrued from the new development and the interest charge payable on a sum borrowed to fund the capital cost of the mains and any other new installations provided. A notable amendment to previous legislation (The Water Act 1945, Section 37) is the facility for the undertaker to include in the financial calculation a reasonable portion, if applicable, of the cost of providing earlier mains capacity (now to be taken up by the new development) in a preceding period of up to twelve years.

Section 42 imposes a duty to connect domestic properties to mains following receipt of a notice from the owner or occupier through the provision of communication pipes at the requisitioner's expense.

Section 43 includes certain conditions imposed upon the requisitioner of a new communication pipe, including payment in advance and compliance with byelaws for 'private' pipework and fittings.

Section 44 stipulates periods of 21 and 14 days respectively for the installation by the undertaker of communication pipes (including ferrule and boundary stop-tap) and mains connections only.

Section 45 contains an obligation to provide water to premises for domestic purposes and to maintain the service connection other than, for instance, when necessary works are being carried out or when the customer fails to pay charges.

Supply for Non-domestic Purposes

Section 46 imposes a duty to supply water for non-domestic purposes, conditional upon the protection of existing domestic and non-domestic supplies.

Supplies for Firefighting etc.

Section 47 requires hydrants to be fixed to distribution mains, and subsequently maintained, at the request and cost of fire authorities or the owner/occupier of any factory or business premises. Water may be taken from any main fitted with a hydrant for the purpose of extinguishing fires.

Section 81 stipulates that water used for firefighting (and any other emergency purpose), the testing of firefighting equipment and the training of firefighting personnel, be provided free of charge.

Supplies for Public Purposes

Section 48 allows water from any main fitted with a hydrant to be used on request, under reasonable terms and conditions, for sewer and drain cleaning, highway watering and in public facilities such as baths and wash houses.

Supply Interruptions and Disconnections

Section 49 confers powers upon the undertaker to cut off a supply of water in the event of the customer's request, his default in the payment of charges or for the purpose of carrying out necessary works. Notice of intent is required in both the latter cases and, where work is being undertaken, there is an obligation to complete within a reasonable time, interruptions in excess of 24 hours necessitating the provision of an alternative temporary supply.

Separation of Services

Reference was made in Chapter 2 to problems commonly encountered in relation to joint supply pipes. Section 50 entitles undertakers to require single exclusive service connections to be made to individual properties under particular circumstances, such as a defect or insufficiency in the existing joint supply, the non-payment of water charges, or significant structural modification to the properties connected.

Constancy and Pressure of Supply

Section 51 requires a sufficient pressure in the mains to feed water by gravity to the top of the topmost storey of every building connected. This pressure is qualified in that it need be no greater than that governed by the supplying service reservoir and that the reservoir concerned be designated by the undertaker.

A requisitioner whose property requires a pressure greater than 10.5 m below the draw-off level of the designated supplying service reservoir is required to install a storage cistern of sufficient volume to provide an adequate supply to the property for a period of twenty-four hours.

Quality of Supply

Section 52 imposes an obligation to provide 'wholesome' water for domestic purposes, wholesomeness being specified through technical standards embodied within the Water Supply (Water Quality) Regulations 1989.

Section 53 refers to these Regulations, in particular the requirement to monitor and to make water quality information available for inspection free of charge.

Section 54 represents an important legislative innovation in that it is deemed a criminal offence to supply water 'unfit for human consumption'.

Section 56 requires local authorities to 'keep themselves informed' about the sufficiency and wholesomeness of water supplied in their areas and to notify the undertaker of problems.

Schedule 22 of the Act contains a supplement to Section 76 of the Water (Scotland) Act 1980 embodying these provisions within the arena of water quality.

Contamination, Waste and Misuse of Water

Section 61 details instances in which owners/occupiers of premises are deemed guilty of an offence.

Section 62 empowers the Secretary of State to make appropriate regulations and empowers representatives of water undertakers or local authorities to enter premises to check for compliance.

51

Section 63 contains powers to serve notice upon offending consumers requiring improvement or preventative measures to be taken. In 'emergency' situations the issue of such a notice may be preceded by a disconnection of supply.

THE PUBLIC UTILITIES STREETWORKS ACT 1950

This legislation provides mutual protection arrangements between the highway authority and the utilities and also between one utility and another.

The Act embodies a system of communications between the highway authority and each utility, and between the utilities themselves, based upon a requirement for the several parties to notify each other of impending works they intend to execute, such notices to be served within a specified time period in advance, variable with the nature of the work.

The production, issuing, receipt and response to and recording of PUSWA notices represents a significant routine daily workload for staff within the distribution function, in particular for mainlaying works where the dimensions of excavations are included in notices served upon the highway authority, later to be used as a checking mechanism when that authority's invoices for the cost of permanent reinstatement are received. In some cases at least part of the process may be computerized, using a variety of available software: future technological and statutory development may prompt consideration of the potential for computerized links between the various bodies involved.

Any future legislative change consistent with many of the recommendations contained in the Horne Report (see Chapter 3, Section 5) will necessitate significant modification to procedures currently dictated by this Act.

2. WATER BYELAWS

LEGAL BACKGROUND

Water undertakers have for many years been empowered in law to make and, where made, given a duty to enforce, byelaws governing the quality, arrangement and usage of pipework and fittings in any installation connected to the public water supply system. (Those powers are replaced in England and Wales by Section 62 of the Water Act 1989, in which the Secretary of State may now make regulations. Pending the introduction of these, existing byelaws and powers under Section 17 of the Water Act 1945 are to continue.)

PURPOSES OF BYELAWS

The purposes of the byelaws are fourfold, with the intention of preventing:

(1) waste;   (2) misuse;
(3) undue consumption; and   (4) contamination.

Undertakers electing to make byelaws have for many years used a national 'model' format as a basis, adapted to suit local circumstances and requirements. The earliest form of model was developed about 1920 in recognition of the undesirability of differing rules and practices applied across the country; more recent legislation has required that byelaws made by individual undertakers, irrespective of any common basis, are submitted to the appropriate government minister for approval prior to implementation.

CURRENT SITUATION

During the 1980s a major national review of the model byelaws was undertaken, its purpose being to reassess priorities and to achieve a greater degree of uniformity of application. New national byelaws came into force on 1st January 1989; their principal features are:

(*a*) a greater emphasis upon the need to prevent contamination through backsiphonage;
(*b*) a recognition of developments in plumbing arrangements at home and in Europe (for example, the unvented hot water system); and
(*c*) a virtually uniform adoption without amendment throughout the UK.

The byelaws cover pipework and fittings used in water-conveying installations but do not extend to the quality or fitness for purpose of materials and products, those aspects being covered by British Standards and other testing and acceptance procedures.

POLICING, INTERPRETATION AND ENFORCEMENT OF BYELAWS

Policing, interpretation and enforcement of the byelaws is a vital aspect of the work of the distribution function, related to new and existing, domestic and commercial, pipework and fittings installations. Few activities within the function are not influenced in some way by the byelaws and it is recommended that staff concerned are equipped with or have ready access to three publications, the byelaws document itself, the Water Supply Byelaws Guide[1] and a current copy of the Water Fittings and Materials Directory[2], the latter two being available also in the form of a microcomputer software package with updating facility.

3. FINANCE

Finance has a high profile in relation to many aspects of the distribution function, which may be expressed under three headings:

(i) income (charges for water, for (where applicable) 'infrastructure' and for work undertaken);
(ii) expenditure (capital investment and operating costs); and
(iii) performance monitoring (measures of efficiency).

WATER CHARGES, MEASURED AND UNMEASURED

Distribution, with its close interface with the customer, demands a high level of understanding of the water charging system, staff concerned being required not only to read meters for the purpose of measured charging but also to gather and interpret information relevant to the application of charges, to respond directly or indirectly to questions raised by the customer, and to resolve queries raised by the billing department.

Income for the provision of water services is raised through charging on either an unmeasured or measured basis, the former presently applicable to most domestic properties, the latter to most industrial and commercial premises.

The annual bill for an unmeasured water supply service is calculated on the basis of a fixed standing charge and a charge per £1 of rateable value of the property served. A minimum cut-off level is normally applied to the water supply bill such that a base level of income is derived from very low rateable value properties. Bills for sewerage services (the removal and treatment of sewage and rainwater) are similarly compiled. Most undertakers exercise their legal right to recover charges by half-yearly or monthly instalments.

Measured charges apply to metered premises, monthly or quarterly meter readings indicating the volume of water consumed which, when multiplied by the current annual rate per cubic metre and added to a standing charge based upon peak consumption (usually indicated by meter size), provides the water charge. Measured sewerage charges are based upon the proportion (say 95 per cent) of water supplied through the meter. Trade effluent charges may be calculated from a proportion of metered water consumption plus an element geared to the effluent strength. Certain water supply and sewerage charges qualify for VAT according to the mode of usage.

The determination of which properties should be charged by which method lay, until the early 1980s, entirely with the water undertaker and was usually decided on a 'maximization of income' basis. Since about 1982 all customers have been able to choose a measured form of charging if desired, known generally as the 'metering option scheme'. Domestic customers had the option also to change from a measured to an unmeasured supply provided that a period of notice, normally twelve months, was given. Non-domestic customers did not enjoy this latter option otherwise than by mutual agreement.

All measured and most unmeasured charges are recovered by 'direct billing', a straightforward transaction between the water undertaker and the customer. In some cases water-related income is derived via the local authority, acting as an agent, through its general rate collection system, an appropriate commission fee being levied upon the undertaker for the service provided. Either party has the right to withdraw from such an arrangement, which may be costly to the undertaker in respect of the commission paid but has the advantage of transferring to the local authority the burden of dealing with arrears. Water undertakers are, however, becoming increasingly conscious of the overall advantages of establishing direct links with the entire spectrum of their customer base.

Introduction of the community charge in lieu of the general rating system in 1990 effectively eliminated the requirement for properties to have a rateable value. The water industry is required therefore to develop an alternative system of charging for currently unmeasured supplies, to be in place by the year 2000. This may involve the introduction of universal metering or some other acceptable form of charging. As part of that decision-making process, domestic metering trials have been carried out at twelve sites in England, comprising eleven small-scale exercises and one large-scale exercise, involving approximately 1000 and 53 000 households respectively. The trials require that customers involved are charged by measure and facilitate experimental tariff arrangements across a range of socio-economic groups.

An interim policy adopted by many undertakers is to install meters to all new domestic properties (there is no longer a necessity for rateable values to be assigned) and to convert all unmetered non-domestic premises to a measured basis of charge.

Another aspect of charging for water is the provision of temporary supplies for construction works, local authority activities and other occasional usage, where there is no applicable rateable value as the basis of charging. A system of standpipe hire is normally used for these purposes. The hirer may be required to lodge a cash deposit sufficient to cover the value of the standpipe and key, refundable upon return of the undamaged items, and then charged at a daily or weekly rate to cover the cost of water usage. When high water usage is considered likely, a metered standpipe may be provided, with cash deposit, but charges for water used calculated on a measured basis.

The abstraction of water from hydrants can cause problems of dirty or discoloured water to properties in the vicinity and it is usual to nominate specific hydrants where the risk of disturbance is considered to be low. Standpipes for hire are often fitted with anti-vacuum or anti-backsiphonage devices to protect against contamination of the mains system. Both measures are of limited benefit, physical surveillance being the most effective form of control, ideal in theory but difficult to achieve in practice.

Whilst it may be tempting to maximize the charges associated with standpipe hire, in compensation for the problems it can cause, its effect may well be to increase the degree of illicit use of hydrants, a practice which is illegal by virtue of the taking of water without charge and equally undesirable from the associated higher risk of contamination. Illicit users are likely to exercise less care in the course of their work, resulting perhaps in hydrant damage or broken chamber covers, a situation of great concern to the Fire Service as the source of funding for the repair and maintenance of most hydrants in the system.

INFRASTRUCTURE CHARGES

The water supply infrastructure upstream of the distribution system (dams, river intakes, boreholes, treatment works, trunk mains) represents works of major capital investment designed to demand projections of up to 20 years, embodying at any given time a degree of 'spare' capacity, available to meet the additional load imposed by new development.

Major works are funded from the charges levied upon existing customers, who in consequence carry the financial burden of this 'spare' capacity, deriving little direct benefit from it.

In order to transfer some of that burden to customers newly-connected to the system (who therefore do derive direct benefit through their take-up of spare capacity) the Water Act 1989 has introduced, in England and Wales, an 'infrastructure charge' to be levied in respect of all new properties taking a 'domestic' supply (which includes non-domestic premises whose supply contains a 'domestic' element, such as kitchens, washrooms etc). The charge also applies to existing property converted into multiple units.

Permitted infrastructure charge limits vary between undertakers, indicative of individual company infrastructure circumstances, and range for 1990/91 from about £110 to £1000.

Infrastructure charges, payable usually in advance of connection of the property, are applied also in respect of sewerage.

RECHARGEABLE WORKS

Another significant source of income generated within the distribution function is that arising from rechargeable works, including new mains where a contribution is required from the developer, mains diversions, fire hydrant installation and maintenance, new communication pipes and modification or maintenance to any 'private' pipework. There are generally three forms of charging used in relation to rechargeable works:

(1) '**actual cost**', following the provision of an original estimate to the customer;
(2) '**firm estimate**' by which the customer knows beforehand exactly how much the work will cost and all the risk of variation is borne by the undertaker; and
(3) '**standard charge**', a tariff system applied to a range of regular and routine jobs, each having a price or price basis equivalent to the cost of the average or typical job of that nature.

It is usual to monitor the costs of standard charge works against income and to compensate for any cash deficit or surplus at the end of the year at the time of inflationary re-pricing.

DEBT RECOVERY

The non-payment of water charges, and in particular the action required to be taken for their recovery, is a contentious issue, the subject of great social and political debate. Uncontrolled arrears can account for 5 to 10 per cent of total turnover and most undertakers have in recent years taken steps to reduce the deficit. Disconnection of supplies has generally increased as a result, although its use is considered very much as a last resort, having first pursued the matter through the courts and checked carefully, in the case of the domestic customer, the personal circumstances of the household concerned. The disconnection process, one of the distribution function's less pleasant activities, normally involves attendance on site of a debt recovery officer, to deal with the customer, together with an inspector to apply a locking device to the boundary stop-tap or, for a more permanent disconnection, a work crew to excavate and disconnect the communication pipe. Where domestic properties are concerned it is usual for the undertaker to inform the local authority (for the attention particularly of the Environmental Health Officer). Supplies are restored upon payment of the outstanding arrears plus a supplementary charge to cover the cost of reconnection.

EXPENDITURE

Traditionally outgoings have been dealt with under two headings, 'revenue' and 'capital'. 'Revenue' expenditure has applied to works or activities of a regular, routine and recurrent nature such as burst repairs, meter reading and service reservoir cleaning, whilst 'capital' has covered, in principle, more major 'one-off' types of work above a certain value, say £3000, such as the provision of a new main or the construction of a pumping station. Distinction between the two has always been blurred; for instance, expenditure on mains renovation (the scraping and internal lining of an encrusted main) could be considered as 'revenue' since the work is essentially maintenance but is normally treated as 'capital' despite there being no additional asset created as a result.

Strict application of economics logic throws up a number of such anomalies and has led to some variation in accounting practices at the margin across the industry. It is essential therefore that the distribution manager knows precisely what is charged where within his own organization as a procedural if not necessarily logical decision-making aspect of his work.

Privatization of the industry in England and Wales has prompted the adoption of the 'infrastructure' method of accounting, aimed at a uniformity of approach and a regime more appropriate to commercial organizations, consistent with the future application of taxation regulations.

Block Allocations for Mains Expenditure

Before leaving the topic of expenditure it is worth considering current practices adopted in relation to the major aspect of capital investment within the distribution function, that associated with mains.

It is usual to adopt a financial ceiling for mains schemes, say £100 000 in value, projects above which are promoted as part of the undertaker's major capital programme. Smaller schemes may be financed through an annual block allocation, the size of which is determined at the beginning of the year from an assessment of likely external demand from new property development and an estimate of the requirements to rectify known problems in the system. The introduction of 'asset management planning' in association with privatization has determined investment requirements for system rehabilitation over future years through a significant extension to the planning horizon.

Capital investment within the block allocation covers a variety of scheme types which may be categorized as:

(a) **Statutory** – the provision of mains to service new domestic or industrial development; or of mains diversions as a result of external construction works.
(b) **Reinforcement** – the laying of new mains to overcome hydraulic deficiency in the system or provide strategic links.
(c) **Renewal** – the replacement of defective mains.
(d) **Renovation** – the refurbishment of defective mains.

The latter two categories are unlikely in the future to be regarded as capital investment.

PERFORMANCE MONITORING

Since the mid 1980s, when much of the industry began to prepare for privatization, operational efficiency has assumed increasing prominence. It is now normal practice for undertakers to compare their relative performance across a range of activities, both externally in relation to each other and internally between organizational divisions or areas, producing a significant impact within operational functions, demanding a high level of cost consciousness among staff involved and requiring a close working relationship between operational and accountancy colleagues.

Performance monitoring is based upon a number of cost/parameter measures which, for the distribution function, may include:

   (i) operating cost per population served;
  (ii) operating cost per length of main;
 (iii) operating cost per volume of water supplied;
 (iv) operating cost per job category (for example, average cost of mains burst repair);
  (v) mainlaying unit costs;
 (vi) employee number per population served; and
(vii) outstanding debt per population served.

4. WORK RESOURCES

Undertakers adopt differing organizational arrangements within the distribution function but in general resources conform to the following grouping:

(1) Administrative   (2) Technical
(3) Supervisory   (4) Inspectorate
(5) Direct labour   (6) External resources.

Space precludes a detailed examination of the activities of each group, although it may be useful to illustrate some features of groups (4) to (6).

THE INSPECTORATE

The use of the term 'inspectorate' is strictly a misnomer since the inspection activity represents only one element of the work involved. The inspectorate, normally uniformed staff, covers a range of duties including:

  (a) **District Inspection**. Responsibility for operating the system within a given district involving valve operations, record keeping, general surveillance, problem-solving and customer liaison.
  (b) **Byelaw Inspection**. Byelaw policing, enforcement, interpretation and advice to customers, builders etc; cost estimation in relation to new services, meters etc.
  (c) **Leakage Control**. Leakage detection surveys; general surveillance; and sounding.

In some cases these duties may be undertaken by inspectors designated 'district', 'byelaw' and 'waste', in others some of the duties may be combined or varied and may extend to the additional roles of meter reading and control room operations.

DIRECT LABOUR

'Multi-skilling'

Most undertakers employ a distribution direct labour force able to execute a range of work embracing mainlaying and maintenance, service laying and maintenance, together with service reservoir cleaning, stores operation and grounds maintenance.

Since 1975 employees within the labour force have been encouraged through training and experience to become multi-skilled across the spectrum of distribution work, reflected in a nationally negotiated and agreed broadbanding schedule, a matrix of tasks grouped by skill or responsibility level to which the various pay classifications are allocated. The erosion of demarcation between, say, mainlaying and service laying has led to greater efficiency through the ability of single, properly equipped crews on site to undertake any work without the necessity to call upon additional or specialist assistance.

Contract Resources

Distribution work can be 'peaky', due to a number of contributory factors such as capital investment adjustments, local development activity and climatic change (winter bursts, for instance). Whilst the use of contract resources for the execution of large or specialist works has always been common practice, their more general deployment on distribution works as a supplement to the direct labour force in a peak-lopping capacity was not, but is now, fairly widespread. It is generally believed that the balanced use of the two forms of resource represents sound managerial practice by dealing adequately with workload peaks, providing the opportunity to continually monitor and compare costs and maintaining an option to increase activity in either respect should contract or direct labour costs rise significantly.

Consultancy Resources

Deployment of external contracted resources in the form of consultants or agency personnel has also increased in recent years to augment in-house staff, usually in the technical field. Short-term to medium-term projects representing a high workload or, on occasions, specific skill, are often executed by this means, for example the design and implementation of network modelling and telemetry schemes.

5. EMERGENCIES

VULNERABILITY OF THE DISTRIBUTION SYSTEM

The industry provides to its customers a 24 hour per day, 365 day per year service in respect of its operational functions. The distribution system represents the most vulnerable element from the frequency of failure and the direct and immediate impact those failures can have upon the customer.

OPERATIONS CENTRES

Normally a divisional or regional operations centre, manned round the clock on a rotating shift arrangement, is designated the focal point for all out-of-hours communications and emergency management. Usually the centre will accommodate telephone and radio communication equipment, telemetry reception and readout facilities and, where available, the means of remotely controlling pumps, valves or other installations.

Since the majority of failures occur within the distribution system these centres are often operated within the distribution function and manned with experienced former distribution field personnel, though required to deal at times with events related to water treatment, sewerage, sewage treatment or pollution.

EMERGENCY STANDBY AND CALLOUT ARRANGEMENTS

Failures in distribution range from minor service pipe leaks to major mains bursts or pump breakdowns affecting large numbers of customers over a wide area. Some incidents do not require attention until the next normal working hours period; others, especially in the major category, necessitate immediate corrective action. For that reason most undertakings operate emergency standby and callout arrangements whereby key groups of personnel undertake, on rotation, a periodic (say weekly) standby system. During the duty period they are available to be telephoned and called out by the shift duty officer to attend the incident. Standby personnel may be provided with a home telephone, a telephone pager or an official vehicle equipped with mobile radio.

Typically the groups forming standby rotas within distribution may comprise inspectors, works supervisors, and repair crews. Their role, depending upon the nature of the incident, may be augmented by other functional groups, operating their own standby systems, such as laboratory staff, treatment operatives, mechanical/electrical craftsmen or even senior managers whose role is to advise in the most difficult cases, act in situations where the incident has serious implications, or to elicit external operational support should the necessity arise.

It is normal practice for standby repair crews to be skilled in all aspects of pipework repair, to be provided with an appropriate vehicle plus tools and equipment, and to carry in the vehicle a range of materials and repair items suitable for the majority of jobs. Larger jobs can warrant the attendance of more than one team and perhaps special arrangements with the stores to ensure quick and easy access to the requisite materials and fittings.

Emergency shift and standby systems can be costly, much of their benefit being of an 'insurance' as well as of a practical application nature. The extent to which cover is provided is a matter largely of judgement, dependent upon a number of factors including system condition, vulnerability, degree of risk and customer sensitivity.

EMERGENCY PROCEDURE

The process of dealing with a failure, for instance a mains burst, generally conforms to the following model:

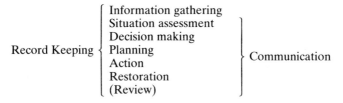

The model represents good practice, most of the steps being self-explanatory but some are worthy of particular mention.

Planning

Planning is, in the heat of the moment, sometimes neglected. Speed is of the essence when dealing with a failure and there is nothing more frustrating than arriving on site with the wrong equipment or materials or suffering from incorrect valve operation in the process of shutting-down or re-zoning.

Action

Action encompasses both the repair work itself and 'damage limitation', the provision of alternative supplies by valve adjustment or the mobilization of standpipes or water bowsers as a means of temporary supply.

Restoration

Restoration includes recharging on completion of the repair (a process which may be time consuming if, for instance, the main has become air-locked) sterilization and perhaps the taking of water samples for analysis if there is considered to have been a significant risk of contamination.

Review

Review, not always an essential step (hence shown in brackets), relates to the more major, significant or perhaps poorly-handled incidents. Analysis of the decisions and actions taken can produce valuable lessons for the future.

Record Keeping

Many incidents, however ultimately serious, begin with the receipt of an apparently minor piece of information. Strict adherence to the discipline of record-keeping from the outset, usually by the duty officer at the operations centre, can prove invaluable later as the situation develops. Once the problem has been established as minor or routine, record keeping can safely be curtailed, but at least the foundation has been laid if needed.

Communication

Communication is probably the single most important feature of the entire process, requiring great attention in respect of all personnel involved or interested in the problem and, most importantly, the customers whose supplies are affected. As well as domestic customers who are inconvenienced, special individual attention may need to be paid to water-reliant industrialists and vital services such as schools, hospitals, home dialysis installations and the Fire Service. Standards of communication with customers whose supplies are interrupted are imposed by regulation upon undertakers in England and Wales.

6. STORES

Stores Management

The distribution function, the major operational consumer of materials and fittings, tends to be home to stores and the issue and recording of virtually all stock items, including those for use by other functions.

Stores management involves the establishment of maximum and minimum stock levels for each item held, the issue of goods and the accompanying reconciliation process, re-ordering, stock-checking and, in general, ensuring that items are always available to sustain work in the field yet minimizing stock levels to achieve maximum economy.

Some commonly-adopted features of stores management are:

(i) **Strategic Stock**. A means of storing important but low-utilization items such as large diameter pipes and fittings for use in the repair of large mains.
(ii) **Emergency Stock**. The storage of repair kits external to the main stores, enabling quick access by repair crews without the necessity to gain entry to the stores building.
(iii) **Imprest Stock**. An arrangement to avoid queuing at the stores counter at peak times such as the beginning of the day. Crew vehicles may be equipped with a semi-secure store of their own for small high-usage items such as plumbing fittings and coils of small diameter pipe.
(iv) **Variety Limitation**. Strictly a purchasing rather than stores policy whereby the types and sizes of each particular item are, as far as possible, standardized. This provides the advantage of enhanced purchasing power and lower prices, and simplifies the physical layout of the stores by minimizing the number of racks or bins required because of the smaller range of items.
(v) **Security**. Most stores take the form of a high-security building with limited access to all but stores personnel, in which smaller or more valuable items are kept, plus an outside storage area for the larger items, including pipes, valves and loose materials such as sand, aggregate and tarmacadam. The outside store is often fenced and provided with vehicular road barriers at the points of entry and exit.

Stores management lends itself well to new technology, so that computerized inventory management systems, automatic fuel dispensers and bar coding are common features of many undertakers' stores operations.

7. THE CUSTOMER

This book ends where it began by focusing upon the close relationship between the distribution function, the people working within it and the customer.

PERCEPTION OF STANDARD OF SERVICE

The nature of the water supply service is unique in that the customer has no option but to use the supplier serving the area in which he resides or works. His perception of the standard of service he receives tends to be either perfect or bad, two extremes with little shade of grey in between. Given this situation it is interesting to examine how customer dissatisfaction is reflected in terms of complaints received.

CUSTOMER COMPLAINTS

Records indicate that typically the total number of customer contacts per year in relation to water supply accounts for about 5 per cent of households and non-domestic premises, less than half of which, on average, are likely to be in the nature of complaints of substandard service such as loss of supply, low flow or poor water quality. This suggests therefore that 98 per cent of all properties receive each year a standard of service which elicits no complaint, or, alternatively, one complaint per property may be expected every 50 years, indicative, apparently, of a very reasonable overall supplier performance. The relationship between standard of service and level of complaint is of course much more complex and less logical than it might seem, being influenced by some of the more psychological aspects of customer behaviour.

Analyses of enquiry statistics and standards provided have been known to reveal that customers may suffer chronic supply problems without complaint. Evidence suggests that change, particularly in the form of a deterioration, is the stimulus to most complaints rather than a poor standard of service *per se*. One example is the case of a new treatment works and associated mains refurbishment scheme which, on commissioning, eradicated severe and long-standing discoloured water problems to some 200 000 customers without any significant consequential reduction in the numbers of complaints received.

It is important therefore to recognize that, to achieve and maintain customer satisfaction, problems to be tackled may extend beyond those which prompt complaint, that standards must be monitored separately from any complaint recording procedure, and that current satisfactory levels of service need to be maintained.

IMPORTANCE OF INFORMATION

The key to the achievement of harmonious customer relations is information. In the context of change the golden rule is, wherever possible, to pre-warn the customer of the nature of the impending change, the reason for it, the action to be taken and the timescale (the principle of 'no surprises'). When change is immediate, for instance as the result of a burst, it is essential to provide the remainder of such information as rapidly as possible. The most difficult complaints to deal with are, without exception, those involving affected customers who are ill-informed; conversely it is amazing the extent to which most customers will readily suffer inconvenience when pre-warned, well informed and updated. Any letters from customers usually contain reference not only to work performance but also to the manner in which the customer has been treated, indicative of a perception of something 'beyond the call of duty'.

WARNING PROCEDURES

The process of warning communication with the customer, for instance where planned work in the system requires a mains shut-off and consequent supply interruption, can involve one or more of the following methods:

(1) Personal contact by visit or telephone (undoubtedly the most effective and appreciated but probably the most time consuming and costly).
(2) Personal letter or postcard, by mail or direct delivery.
(3) By the press or media (less than 100 per cent coverage).
(4) By mobile loud hailer (less than – or more than – 100 per cent coverage; a 'last resort' option when time is short).

Common practice for planned work is to pre-warn customers where possible to a specific notice period, say 48 hours for domestic supplies and 7 days for non-domestic. Industrial users dependent upon a constant supply sometimes find interruptions during working hours unacceptable to the extent that they are prepared to cover the cost of overtime working if the job can be re-scheduled to night-time or the weekend.

WATER SUPPLY REGULATIONS

Privatization of the industry in England and Wales has had a significant impact upon customer knowledge and perception and has formalized certain of these good practices through the introduction, in relation to domestic customers, of The Water Supply and Sewerage Services (Customer Service Standards) Regulations 1989. The regulations dictate the speed of response to enquiries and complaints and the type of warning information provided in association with supply interruptions and entitle the customer to claim the sum of £5 per day in the event of non-compliance.

The Director General of Water Services requires also that *inter alia* undertakers publish, as part of their 'Instruments of Appointment' (Licences), Codes of Practice for domestic customers covering:

(*a*) customers (nature of services, tariffs, payments, complaints, meter testing, emergencies, and the functions of the Customer Service Committee);
(*b*) supply disconnection procedures; and
(*c*) leakage on customer supply pipes.

Undertakers are obliged in addition to comply with the Director General standards of service and to provide regular performance information to him against those standards. Two in which the Director General has expressed particular interest (significant in distribution) are:

(i) pressure of mains water; and
(ii) unplanned interruptions to supply.

Customer Service Committees, referred to above, one each per undertaker, represent the interests of the customer and have direct access to the Director General.

RESPONSIBILITIES TO THE CUSTOMER

As mentioned earlier, the perception which the customer has of the performance of the entire organization is founded upon the treatment and courtesy he experiences from those with whom he has contact, in most cases distribution staff. 'Front line' personnel, whether telephonist, technician, supervisor, inspector, operative or manager, need to be aware not only of their responsibilities in relation to the standard of service, the cost of providing it and (where applicable) the need for regulatory compliance, but also to the added dimension of customer care, attention to which can both ease the burden of an operational problem and reduce the ultimate cost of its resolution.

8. REFERENCES

1. WATER RESEARCH CENTRE (Water Byelaws Advisory Service), *The Water Supply Byelaws Guide* (S. F. White and G. D. Mays, Eds.), WRc with Ellis Horwood, 1989.

2. WATER RESEARCH CENTRE, *The Water Fittings and Materials Directory* (G. D. Mays, Ed.), Martins Publishers (twice annually).

Additional Bibliography
3. MACRORY, R., *The Water Act 1989, Text and Commentary*, Sweet and Maxwell, London, 1989.

Index